40 years

BSCOS

British Society for Children's
Orthopaedic Surgery

1984-2024

BSCOS – The first 40 years

The British Society for Children's Orthopaedic Surgery

– the first 40 years

Edited by
Simon L Barker MD

BSCOS – The first 40 years

Contents

BSCOS – The first 40 years

Introduction

In some ways children's orthopaedic care is as old as the hills, and the children who injured themselves whilst running around on them. It is speculated that splintage of fractures may date back to the stone age, based largely on evidence of aligned fracture unions in preserved specimens. Spinal deformities including kyphosis and scoliosis were named by Hippocrates, four hundred years before Christ. In human terms, ours is an ancient discipline.

Yet in other ways we are a relatively young area of subspecialist practice. The British Orthopaedic Association itself was founded in 1894. Before that, the entirety of Orthopaedic practice had been a fragment, albeit a significant part, of an increasingly unwieldy collective of 'general surgery'. We are still, just, within living memory of a generalist surgeon who would attend to your abdomen alongside your femur and in some remote parts of the British Isles this pattern of care persists. The echoes of that age persist in the form of Royal

Colleges which still straddle the full diversity of the surgical spectrum in the face of members who practice a small and often still shrinking aspect of it.

The drive toward subspecialisation was for a time comfortably accommodated in the BOA tent when most Orthopaedic Surgeons were at most doing a (small) component of paediatric practice alongside their more sizeable adult commitments. Many of us can recall a time when 'generalist' orthopaedic surgeons would tackle most anything that came their way. Indeed, our training programmes are still directed toward the goal of producing competency in the generality of trauma and orthopaedic surgery at the award of a certificate of completion of training. Few, if any now, persist in such a breadth of practice thereafter. The expectation is of development of a subspecialist interest with fellowship(s) to support that.

It took ninety years from the inception of the BOA for the unique orthopaedic needs of children to be fully recognised in the founding of our society. We can readily recognise parallel developments in other subspecialty societies within and indeed beyond the Orthopaedic diaspora both in the United Kingdom and overseas. Specifically in children's orthopaedics the awareness of paediatric focussed care in Orthopaedics coalesced internationally in the 1980s. It's no accident that both POSNA and EPOS arose at a similar time to BSCOS.

The fruits of this increased professional specificity have been yielded in an increased focus on paediatric aspects of orthopaedic training and education.

Moreover, in the last decade we have seen significant NIHR funding in the UK enable rigorous scientific method to be applied at scale on disabling child specific conditions that as Orthopaedic surgeons we each see in small number. This has been paralleled with the advent of enhanced and large scale genetic alongside more traditional epidemiological methodology to elucidate causality, narrowing the utility of the term 'idiopathic' slowly but surely to a dwindling but persistent cohort of conditions. The curtain is being pulled back from skeletal dysplasias and metabolic presentations at pace. Equally, large scale studies now underway promise evidence based answers for management conundrums including Legg Calve Perthes disease, Slipped Upper Femoral Epiphysis, and Hip Dysplasia amongst others.

BSCOS has always been a friendly society with an emphasis on candour, encouraging learning through each other's experiences, errors and achievements. Many of us recognise the superlative educational value of scrutinising, with kindness, our failures on the road to success. My own heroes are not those who have claimed perfection, but in humility have advanced our understanding with honesty about their struggles and challenges. It's a core aspect of BSCOS that we maintain that openness as we learn together. This authenticity is no small feat in the face of illogical demands for 'everyone to perform above average'. In a climate of clamour for perfection at all times we would do well to guard our safe space for critical collective self-reflection.

In recent years our society has been at the forefront of recognising and acting on historically embedded attitudes which may limit and obstruct opportunity. We've sought to ensure our structures bring a diverse and inclusive perspective to our leadership, the decisions we make, and the aspirations we project into the future of our subspecialty. Conscious rebalancing of previously unchallenged 'norms' receives our ongoing attention as we look to do everything we can to be a diverse and inclusive society which is welcoming to all with an interest in the care of children with bone and joint problems.

That the covid 19 pandemic tested everyone's resolve is an understatement. As we lamented enforced separation and suspension of in-person activities, our society still worked hard to ensure appropriate advice was available to  members, with support for novel ways of delivering care. Our public information videos, for example, reached a wide international audience.

The learning experience of a pandemic was far from entirely negative: it has encouraged us to adopt many more online and hybrid-based activities than we would have previously considered. These have brought inclusivity to members of the society who may be unable to travel easily, have had a positive impact on the society's travel expenses, as well as being friendly to the planet. Nevertheless, the enthusiasm to meet in person remains as strong as ever and our scientific meetings have never been busier since we resumed face to face gatherings.

Through our new structures we are learning to be more responsive to our members, to reach out to colleagues in other disciplines who have an interest in paediatric orthopaedics, and to our patients and their parents, and ever more widely as we interact with those who govern and administer health services. In addition to the Board, we now have committees responsible for leading us forward on educational content, communication and research.

With almost 400 of us now, it's a far cry from 12 members back at the first meeting but it is upon their shoulders that we reach further than ever.

In 2024 the British Society for Children's Orthopaedic Surgery celebrates its fortieth anniversary since inception. This is a timely opportunity for our Society to look back with gratitude to our forebears and look forward with confidence to the future of our specialty and the care we provide.

In short, it's an exciting time to be a children's orthopaedic surgeon and a proud moment to be your colleague and a member of BSCOS.

Simon Barker
BSCOS President, 2022-2024.

The 'prehistoric' period

'Orthopaedia: or the Art of Correcting and Preventing Deformities in Children by Such Means as May be Put into Practice by Parents Themselves and All Such as are Employed in Educating Children'.

Nicolas Andry, 1741.

There was a time before BSCOS!

Our 'parent specialty' of Orthopaedics was of course etymologically defined and derived from the Greek to be at its core about the 'straightening' [ortho-] of children [-paedic]. In 1741 Nicolas Andry, who was Senior Dean of the *Faculty of Physick* in Paris, coined the term in a prescient lay-persons guide to treating

deformity. The front of his book *Orthopédie* complete with an engraving of a splinted deformed tree gave origin to a world-wide and lasting symbol for Orthopaedics as a discipline as well as a descriptive noun for our practice.

Subsequent appropriation of the term 'Orthopaedics' to describe the treatment of all age group musculoskeletal pathology has driven a tautological necessity for us in children's practice. We have had to further define ourselves to be about 'straightening children'...*in children* by adopting the title 'Paediatric Orthopaedic Surgeons'.

Though the phrase 'paediatric orthopaedics' remains a common term, our own Society's preference for the moniker 'Children's orthopaedics' perhaps hints at the friendliness we espouse as a society and has been acknowledged to be a clearer way to express our raison d'etre by our colleagues across the pond (Wenger, 2006 [ISBN 10 0-9779151-0-7]). It is also surely more understandable to the lay person.

Our earliest post-Renaissance forbears can be identified as the 'bonesetters' of the late 1500s, culminating perhaps most famously with Hugh Owen Thomas (1834-1891) who hailed from Anglesey off the coast of North Wales and practised in Liverpool. His invention of the Thomas Splint is perhaps his most famous and life saving legacy amongst many others. Other luminaries of early Orthopaedic care in the United Kingdom must include Syme (1799-1870) of amputation fame, Little (1810-1894) for his work on clubfoot and his establishment of the specialty of Orthopaedics in England, and MacEwan's (1848-1924) pioneering work on osteotomy for deformity. That their work had at least some rationale to support it is perhaps all the more amazing in that it arose at a time when much of medicine was still embedded in quackery. Arsenic, bloodletting and mystical beliefs in spa therapies abounded. We were waiting for the scientific method to replace anecdote and intuition. Yet there was still some patience required, for evidence-based medicine with randomised controlled trials only came into play less than 30 years before the inception of BSCOS.

It's noteworthy that one of the most significant moments in the whole history of surgery concerns a paediatric orthopaedic case.

It was on August 12th, 1865, at Glasgow Royal Infirmary that the 38y old Professor of Surgery, one Joseph Lister, building on the work of Semmelweis, came to treat an eleven year old boy named Joseph Greenlees for a compound tibial fracture sustained when a cartwheel had rolled over him. Carbolic acid dressings were applied. Healing ensued, and the boy was said to be walking again on a sound limb six weeks later (one presumes he was still limping a little at that stage, and not back to running amok but the point is well made nevertheless). Whilst trivial in modern terms, this moment marked the start of antiseptic surgery.

The expectation of infection and death following a wound would be reversed by the introduction of Lister's Carbolic Spray and the possibility of elective surgery was essentially born out of this development. It was for the brave, the desperate and the fool to volunteer for surgery prior to this revelation. Who would want to run the very high risk of succumbing to infection unless forced to do so by circumstance?

The twentieth century honour roll brings us to Watson Jones, Lloyd Roberts, Dennis Brown and then to John Fixsen, Tony Catterall and their contemporaries.

Of course, all the developments we recognise in paediatric orthopaedics are inevitably part of a greater tale of improving anaesthesia, antisepsis, antibiosis, imaging and material science delivering ever greater opportunity to intervene positively in the disabilities and deformities that present for our care.

It behoves us today to recognise much that we take for granted has necessarily relied on the pioneers who cleared the ground and built a strong evidence-based foundation for current practice. To them this volume is dedicated in appreciation.

There are many unsung heroes in our field who get no mention here – their contributions are nevertheless the solid foundation we build upon alongside those who have had more prominent roles.

Surgical subspecialisation within orthopaedic surgery only commenced in the 1980s although general orthopaedic surgeons continued to treat children, particularly their fractures.

The European Paediatric Orthopaedic Society (EPOS) was formed in 1981 and the Pediatric Orthopaedic Society of North America (POSNA) in 1984. Children's orthopaedics as a distinctive subspecialty emerged in the United Kingdom with the founding of the BSCOS, also in 1984 primarily through the vision of Anthony Catterall. He sought to bring together those whose special interest was the management of conditions specific to children.

The first BSCOS meeting in the United Kingdom involved twelve orthopaedic surgeons with a particular interest in children's orthopaedics. From these small beginnings the Society has flourished and now has over 350 members (220 of whom are Paediatric Orthopaedic Surgeons, with the balance including specialty, staff and associate specialist colleagues, doctors in training, allied health professionals and medical students).

For us no less than other scientific disciplines we echo Isaac Newton's refrain: 'If I have seen further [than others], it is by standing on the shoulders of giants'.

BSCOS – The first 40 years

The Early Years

BSCOS, like its sister US & Canadian society POSNA (The Pediatric Orthopedic Society of North America), was founded in 1984. In parallel at this time, John Sharrard (Sheffield) and Henri Bensahel (Paris) are credited with the development of EPOS (the European Paediatric Orthopaedic Society).

The year 1984 conjures up Orwellian images of the collapse of societal freedoms and indeed there are events of that year that haunt us down through the ages. There was famine in Ethiopia, the assassination of Indira Gandhi, and a 12 month long socially divisive miner's strike here in the UK. Yet it was also the year of Band Aid, the first time Virgin Atlantic took flight and, amazingly, the first Apple Mac went on sale. Petrol cost £1.87 a gallon, not a litre. The average UK house price was just £39,000 and a pint of beer was 72 pence. These facts reconjure a world that seems long past and remarkably different to the one we live in today. It was into an unlikely world of *Ford escorts* on the road and

Ghostbusters at the cinema that BSCOS was born.

The inception of our specialist society owes everything to the vision of our founders, and most particularly the efforts of Tony Catterall who is recognisably the driving force for our existence and indeed was our first Secretary.

In time, children's orthopaedics would come to be recognised by the General Medical Council as a defined subspecialty of orthopaedic and trauma care, with recognition in the curriculum for specially training as an essential component for the award of a certificate of completion of training required to enter into substantive consultant practice in the UK. It's hard for those of us in children's orthopaedics today to imagine a world where this idea was novel yet our forebears demonstrated great foresight in laying the path for us back then.

Sadly, much of our archive has been lost over the years but we do know that a meeting to found the Society was held in the Charing Cross hospital in December 1984.

Tony Catterall reflected: *'there had been a feeling among many colleagues that we should set up a specialist group as other specialties had been doing. I cannot remember all the people who came but they included Sharrard, Fixsen, Mckibbin, Wilkinson, Harrison, Colton, Evans, myself and others. We were 12 in all. The subject was the Child's foot. In a general discussion at the end of the papers we agreed that we would set up the society. I was to be the secretary, and I held this office until I became president which I think was in 1992.'*

Our founder members included:

Tony Catterall	London
Keith Tucker	Norwich
John Fixsen	London
Peter Witherow	Bristol
Jon Wilkinson	Southampton
Mike Benson	Oxford
John Sharrard	Sheffield

Their crucial collective realisation was that the orthopaedic care of children was more than an add on to adult care, but deserving of focussed and particular attention in its own right.

A second meeting was held at Great Ormond Street in 1985, hosted by John Fixsen. At this meeting our founders agreed the society's name to be 'BSCOS' and appointed Tony Catterall as secretary.

The first President was John Fixsen, who was followed by John Sharrard and then followed Tony Catterall in 1992. John Clegg took over as Secretary from Tony Catterall at that point.

John Fixsen (1934-2014), First President of BSCOS

From 1985 meetings were held biannnually, each hosted by a member of the society in their own hospital's postgraduate facilities. These low cost events enabled exchange of scientific ideas, presentation of research, practical case based discussion on the management of children's orthopaedics and the development of a network of strong social bonds that have underpinned our society's friendliness down the years.

In 1990 at a meeting in Norwich, Keith Tucker reminisced that a total of ten hotel rooms were booked in the 'Nelson Hotel'. An almighty storm rocked the city and threatened the arrival of members, yet they were made of determined stuff and everyone made it, if only by 4am in one case.

Keith reflected that:
'a huge attraction of the early days was being able to bring along details of a case that was going to be of interest to all and where a collective collegiate opinion was desired.'

It's noteworthy that this earliest goal of the society remains a high priority for current members at our annual scientific meetings.

1994 Meeting of the Society in Sheffield

Combined meetings have been held with sister paediatric orthopaedic surgical societies in mainland Europe and visiting lecturers have been invited to the Society from throughout the world. Recently we have looked to deepen friendships with other paediatric orthopaedic societies by joint webinars and exchange visits.

Whilst our singular focus is and will ever remain paediatric orthopaedic care, we necessarily recognise that BSCOS remains part of a broader Orthopaedic discipline. To this end we are a

31

member of the Board of Specialist Societies of the BOA. It is here that we exchange ideas with the broader specialty of Orthopaedics, and contribute to consultations and health policy that impacts on our work.

The Middle Ages

For its first 30 years the Society thrived and slowly grew around its single day meetings that were held in the Winter and Summer each year. These were conducted at minimal cost, often free to attendees in those early years, with thrifty use of hospital venues by local hosts.

The Board of the Society was singularly responsible for organisation of society activities and served us well in those nascent years.

There is an understandable fondness and nostalgia in many more senior society members for those halcyon homespun days where everything came together with seemingly little effort.

Yet there is a cost to success. We were growing in number, growing in demand for resources specific to children's orthopaedic surgery, and growing in diversity. How to satisfy the expanding yet reasonable expectations of our members became a challenge. Conversations emerged around how much we might grow. To what extent should we change? There was nervousness that we might lose what we already had.

The mid 2010s can be rightly identified as a transition point for us from youth to middle age as a Society.

First, under the leadership of James Robb, we became a company limited by guarantee. BSCOS had legal standing for the first time. This signalled a change in emphasis, a necessary emergence from an era of informality. Nevertheless, we have striven to retain the fraternal friendliness that characterised our society from the very start.

A combination of factors, including most notably a burgeoning scientific programme and a desire for a collective evening social event led to our first two-day annual meeting in Aberdeen in 2014. We were no longer fleeing homeward at 4pm, rather continuing to build friendships and swinging each other round in a Ceilidh dance into the night.

James Robb (President) is Piped into the Dinner

International guests in 2014 – the late Fred Dietz (Iowa), Charles Mehlman (Cincinnati) & Peter Armstrong (Shriners).

This was a period of significant growth in attendance at our meetings, exceeding the 100 and then the 200 delegate thresholds.

The days of local hosts coordinating our scientific meetings on their own were now numbered, though we did not guess so at the time. Simply, dealing with the payments, dietary requests, queries, speakers, venue hire, catering, AV, programme printing and so on required to host a 2-day scientific meeting became increasingly unwieldy for the willing volunteer, who was also inevitably a full-time children's orthopaedic surgeon.

The Board was increasingly stretched by a burgeoning agenda, seeking to meet the needs of members, to lead our discipline forwards, and to expand our education and research efforts. The idea of subcommittees was in gestation.

It was during this period that the Society most actively explored the idea of registries. We recognised a growing trend, exemplified most clearly in our arthroplasty colleagues, toward routine collection of patient related data in specified conditions. Societal expectations of increased transparency, if not scrutiny, in healthcare were clearly demonstrated in the emergence of a flurry of rating systems such as 'iwantgreatcare.org' and 'doctify'.

The idea of large databases met with mixed response amongst our members. Whilst we would all recognise the importance of identifying areas for (self) improvement, the effective identification of outliers which have an adverse impact on patient care proved far from straightforward. Who could arbitrate in areas of very limited evidence, whether one approach was inherently worse rather than just different to another? Ultimately the sheer complexity and workload involved with the proposed registries in paediatric orthopaedics was its undoing. Our experiment with large scale registries was paused. In retrospect, it was always going to be a 'tall order' for our specialty. Unlike other subspecialties, we are not performing, for the most part, highly routine and often systematised procedures in paediatric orthopaedics. Most of us undertake a wide smorgasbord of procedures, each in small volume. This variety of practice does not lend itself to the large volume driven funnel plots beloved of arthroplasty colleagues. We are inevitably bunched at the wide mouth of the funnel for small numbers of cases where confidence is low.

Outcome measurements specific to one or two conditions (or procedures) are forever plagued by the problem that there are none that encompass the practice of all (or even the vast majority) of paediatric orthopaedic surgeons. Our diverse practice is both a source of fascination and curse of our sub-specialty.

This is not to suggest a disinterest in collecting data on our part - quite the opposite, as evidenced by burgeoning research activity in our discipline. Yet it seems likely we may need to focus our future efforts around patient reported outcome measures (PROMs) that offer generic results that we can meaningfully compare across the widely variability of specific conditions rather than a gamut of individual measures we could employ for the huge range of small volume individual conditions and treatments we encounter and perform.

We have though seen one area of triumph in the registry 'arena', namely the CPIPS/CPIPEW databases whereby the most common neuromuscular condition we face now has nationwide hard data recorded on a regular basis. In time we are likely to see other specific conditions that are seen in significant number, for example congenital talipes equinovarus, recorded in a registry.

The focus on quality in our practice remains unrelenting and has driven our Society from the very start. How it manifests in a given moment does seem to be a more moveable feast.

Recent years

From a handful to several dozen to several hundred attendees, the annual scientific meetings of the Society have remained the centrepiece of our member-focused activities.

The place for a conference organising company to partner the work was ever more evident until recently it became an absolute necessity when running a meeting online during the pandemic.

With great disappointment the meeting of 2020, due to take place in Manchester, had to be abandoned. This was only the second time ever since our inception that a meeting had to be called off (the only other time was a rail strike in 1995). It fitted the mood of the moment, when life in general seemed to be suspended for a season.

As the coronavirus restrictions became a settled reality we were forced online in 2021 for a meeting that, whilst lacking personal contact, enabled some sense of ongoing interaction and professional development. It was a 'better than expected and much better than nothing' experience and taught us what was possible under the constraints of the pandemic as well as opening our eyes to the possibilities of online teaching. Certainly as a Board we were relieved that members engaged with the online platform so willingly.

There was nevertheless great relief in 2022 when Tonbridge Wells were able to host us in person once more with a meeting at full capacity.

A return to in-person meetings in 2022 at Lingfield Park

It has also been in recent years that the Society has responded to requests from Allied Health Professionals who have a specific interest in children's orthopaedic conditions; for an opportunity to gather as a group under the BSCOS umbrella.

We recognise that we remain principally an organisation for medical practitioners, being the only focal point for Children's Orthopaedic Surgery in the UK; nevertheless we have sought to accommodate specialist nurse, physiotherapist and other health care professionals at our conferences, welcoming their attendance, and most specifically facilitating their own breakout meetings. This development has been to our mutual benefit as we have latterly seen AHP colleagues contributing to enrich our Consensus groups, for example.

An important role in encouraging the next generation of children's orthopaedic surgeons has been highlighted by increasing numbers of vacancies in our subspecialty. In our 2022 workforce survey, 51 centres who responded reported a total of 45 whole time equivalent Consultant vacancies across the UK, with 1/3 of centres facing an unsustainable long term staffing situation. The drivers for these workforce issues are largely outwith the Society's control, however they certainly impact those of us struggling to sustain services and have spurred us on to introduce more educational content, both in person and online, alongside trainee bursaries and mentorship programmes to promote our subspecialty to our future colleagues.

Whilst training grade membership has been available for some time, interest from some medical students led to a new membership category for them alongside developments to raise the profile of paediatric orthopaedics even at this early stage in their careers.

As the society has grown, as meetings have become more complex. As the work of the society has expanded, the Board came over time to perceive the need to cast a wider net, to harness the skills of a wider group of Society members to deliver on an increasingly ambitious agenda. Happily, expanding those involved in taking our Society forward coincided well with our increasing recognition for inclusion and diversity to be realised in leadership within the Society. In short, our subcommittees were born.

Whilst the Board of the Society retains a strategic role, the advent of our subcommittees expands and empowers members of our society to take the lead in key areas to deliver for the future.

The Educational subcommittee

Throughout its history to date, the Society has always placed a very high priority on education, both of surgeons in practice and those who will follow in our footsteps.

This commitment is evidenced in publications to which BSCOS has significantly contributed – for example, the BOA Blue Book for children's fractures, since 2006 and for infection, since 2012.

The education and training priority was formalised in the formation of the first standing subcommittee of the society to focus on this aspect of our work.

As part of the Society's effort to address the educational needs of members and future colleagues, annual bursaries are offered to Consultants, Orthopaedic trainees, Allied health professionals and medical students.

Educational content is prioritised throughout the year including at our annual scientific meetings, current concept courses, sponsorship of BOA paediatric educational sessions, and more recently in online content. This generated our first online medical student teaching event in 2023 as well as a very well received first 'hands on' pre-conference workshop at our Southampton meeting.

Our Education subcommittee comprises enthusiastic educators from amongst our membership who spearhead this ongoing effort.

In 2022 the Society resolved to extend its educational effort to the patient and parent population we serve. The development of patient information leaflets is a significant commitment to this work.

Perhaps the most important role of the education committee looking forward will be to oversee the development of an ever increasing portfolio of online content working alongside local hosts through annual meetings, current concepts courses, and BSCOS sponsored content in our contribution to BOA meetings which extends our reach to a wider audience of colleagues for whom paediatric practice is but a minor component.

The following page summarises the BSCOS strategy for education developed in 2023 which seeks to bring together efforts to offer year-round opportunities that will showcase our subspecialty to medical students and foundation years and develop skills in specialty trainees as well as driving our ongoing CPD as consultants.

BSCOS – The first 40 years

TARGET GROUP	SPRING	SUMMER	AUTUMN	WINTER	FELLOWSHIPS
Patients - PILs (Intoe, Gen val, curly toes, Ganglion & Pop cysts)					
Medical Students - Social media - BOMSA UKMSA links - Elective links - Videos - Slide sets for local meetings/ surgical societies?	'Bring a student' initiative [Annual meeting opportunity to present breakout session]		Online event (1ˢᵗ in 2023)		x1
FY & CT - Taster weeks - Fellowship links - BOTA link?	[Annual meeting opportunity to present breakout session]				
ST - Focus on y3-5 - Core competency modules for local delivery (FIN, Elbow #, Deformity, Osteotomy, Gait)? - BOTA link? - Network of trainees & fellows	Leeds AO Course [Annual meeting free papers]	Sheffield 'SPOTS'	Alder Hey Revision West Mids Revision BOA Friday 'Paeds for all' (practical skills) Webinars		x1
Fellows - Peer review process? - Accreditation RCSED? - Survey/gather intel	[Annual meeting free papers]		CCC (2026)	IPOS	X1 Gwyn Evans X2 Orthopediatric
'Early Years' consultants	Podcast	Podcast	CCC (2026) Podcast	BSSCP Podcast	
Mid-career onward consultants	Annual Scientific Meeting EPOS POSNA	Sheffield Knee Meeting Cardiff Graf Course	CCC (2026) Sheffield Masterclass Global Clubfoot masterclass BOA Thursday Reval trauma session + Jt specialty session	BSSCP Glasgow Graf Course	x2
AHPs	Annual Scientific Meeting (+breakouts)			[BSSCP]	x1

A career in Children's Orthopaedics ?

It's never too soon (and rarely too late) to start on the journey towards working with us in paediatric orthopaedic surgery. Many of us can testify to our own seminal moment very early in our professional careers as house officers (FYs in new money) or before that as medical students, when we discovered our love for and fascination with this area of subspecialist practice.

For the interested medical student, our website will be a great place to start for resources that will help you to learn more about our subspecialty as well as highlighting collaborative events with BOMSA (the British Orthopaedic Medical Students' Association, https://www.bomsa.org.uk).

A key early milestone in your career in children's orthopaedic surgery is to identify a mentor – a locally based paediatric orthopaedic surgeon from the list of BSCOS members on the website. Seek them out and explain your interests to them. No one is expecting a lifetime commitment from you, we love our work and are a friendly group and will respond positively to students and trainees who want to explore the possibilities of working alongside us. If that seems too daunting, do contact the educational committee of BSCOS by email – we will certainly point you in the direction of friendly colleagues who will be happy to meet with you.

Having someone to mentor you who has been through the process of becoming a consultant in your field of interest is truly invaluable. They can guide you in how you might gain experience and in ways to get more involved. Consistently demonstrating your commitment to an area of practice as you undertake audit projects, perhaps help with more formal research, and build skills in clinical settings can only help you when it comes to job applications later.

It's worth bearing in mind that stereotypes of surgical careers that imply no hope of a family life and a terrible work life balance are largely historical. There are diverse routes through training now, with opportunities to modify plans along the way. Less than full time training is now a mainstream route, not a novelty. Whilst a career in paediatric orthopaedics requires commitment to an exacting training, this is not in a formulaic way. The time it takes to complete training is far less important than the competencies that are delivered by the end of it. We are all, in any event, involved in life-long learning – there is no room for the idea of an end to growth of our understanding at the completion of formal training. Paediatric orthopaedic surgeons never stop critically appraising their own practice and seeking to improve. It's part of the privilege and challenge of the job.

So, for the medical student who wonders if this might be the thing for them, why not seek out your local friendly children's orthopaedic surgeon. Ask them if you can join them in clinic, and scrub into some interesting cases with them. You may soon find yourself wielding screwdrivers and mallets as you assist in surgeries. Make a point of maximising what you get out of clinics – they are a rich vein of opportunities to learn. Ask if you can help with an audit project – there will always be one that you can either do yourself or help with. Presenting the results of that project at departmental meetings or even at BSCOS(!) is invaluable experience for the future.

Passing your exams and emerging with MBBS or MBChB from your university is arguably the biggest academic milestone of all. Whatever other interests you have, don't compromise on passing finals!

Foundation years 1 & 2 will be busy, a time to consolidate your medical school learning into actually taking responsibility for clinical situations and decisions. You will likely be very busy, yet there are still great opportunities to build your interests. There are often research projects that you can get involved in – ask the Specialty Trainees you are working alongside who will often be glad of a volunteer to join them in research they are leading on.

Working as a team alongside your FY colleagues with efficient time management should mean you can attend some preferred theatre lists and clinics and so continue to explore your area of interest and demonstrate it tangibly in your CV. Your Educational/Clinical Supervisor, and, if you have maintained contact, your mentor; will be able to help you work out how best to do this.

After FY years an important decision point is reached. To continue to pursue an interest in paediatric orthopaedic surgery will require application to a Trauma and Orthopaedic Training Programme. These involve (in England, Wales and Northern Ireland) a competitive application process to enter 'Core' Specialist Training which is for 2 years (CT1-2) and then further competitive entry to 'Higher' Specialist Training for a further 6 years (ST3-8).

In Scotland the training is delivered on a 'run through' basis whereby competitive entry to

Core and Higher Specialist training is rolled together without interruption (ST1-8).

In early specialty training (whether CT1-2 or ST1-2) there is a requirement to pass the MRCS examinations part A & B which demonstrates a broad range of surgical knowledge across the range of surgical specialties.

At the end of a total of 8 years of satisfactory core &/or specialty training *and* having passed the Intercollegiate FRCS(Tr&Orth) exit examination, the award of Certificate of Completion of Training is made. Formal training is completed, and the newly qualified specialist is eligible for entry to the GMC Specialist Register and to apply for Consultant posts.

During the Specialty training period there are some core competencies that are identified in the trauma and orthopaedic syllabus that are specific to paediatric orthopaedic surgery. Most trainees will spend at least 3 but preferably 6 months in a paediatric orthopaedic attachment during years ST3-8 where they will gain exposure to a range of paediatric orthopaedic pathology, but with a particular aim to support the competencies necessary for day 1 as a consultant who will face children with injuries as part of their trauma on call responsibilities.

As with other areas of subspecialist practice, there has been a growing recognition over time that the skills required to deliver an elective paediatric orthopaedic practice (as well as advanced trauma skills) cannot be acquired in a 3- or 6-month ST attachment to a paediatric orthopaedic department. For those wishing to subspecialise, requests to training programme directors for more time in paediatric orthopaedic surgery during training are often viewed sympathetically subject to fulfilling all the other criteria required to complete training. Even then there is a need for more focussed training. For this reason, toward the end of formal training there is a general expectation that ongoing postgraduate fellowship training will be undertaken for those who wish to subspecialise in paediatric orthopaedic surgery. Six-month, twelve month, or even longer periods in post CCT fellowships where specific skills are honed are now the norm, and will feature in 'essential' categories of person specifications in paediatric trauma and orthopaedic roles.

Educational Supervisors, Training Programme Directors and Mentors will all be happy to help with identifying suitable fellowships. BSCOS is also happy to provide a list of possibilities.

BSCOS is here to support the career journey of all paediatric orthopaedic surgeons, from the earliest inklings of interest perhaps in medical school through training to fellowships and on into the early, mid, and late career stages of consultant practice.

To read more about Specialist Training programmes in the UK:
JCST - https://www.jcst.org
BOA advice - https://www.boa.ac.uk/careers-in-t-o.html
NHS England –
https://www.healthcareers.nhs.uk/explore-roles/doctors/roles-doctors/surgery/trauma-and-orthopaedic-surgery
Training in Scotland –
https://www.scotmt.scot.nhs.uk

The Research subcommittee

We can trace an emerging trend in orthopaedic research through recent years in our society.

In the nineties and earlier, research was largely confined to individual centres and indeed individual clinicians pursuing their own interests. Papers delivered at Society meetings were a final common pathway for these efforts. Indeed, these continue to draw debate and discussion, still forming core content, though perhaps occupying less time within the meeting than they once did.

In the 2000's for reasons we will return to, there came something of a sea-change. Not that we eschew the efforts of the enthusiast who may yet continue to show us truths we feel foolish to have missed for ourselves. Yet, the realisation that we are a specialty of many conditions presenting in small numbers to any one of us, drives an important logic. To pursue answers, we need research at scale, multicentre research is the money hungry way to achieve the numbers that would otherwise take generations to gather.

Our research committee's first big task was to engage with the James Lind Alliance to identify the most important questions to which we needed answers. Tim Theologis perceived the need for and indeed led this vital step, and through it crafted a metaphorical key to unlock funding for our subspecialty.

Since then, we have seen a blossoming of large scale trials, happily greeted with enthusiasm by us all, eager for answers to long standing questions that vex our practice.

The committee regularly update our society on the latest developments and progress with studies. More recently we have also been able to award some pump-priming grants to members with specific research goals.

Alongside education, promoting excellence in research is a core function of BSCOS, the research committee supports members who are seeking grants and with advice on collaborations. We have been ably championed in this endeavour by our research doyen, Dan Perry. Significant projects are now highlighted in a regularly updated research guide:

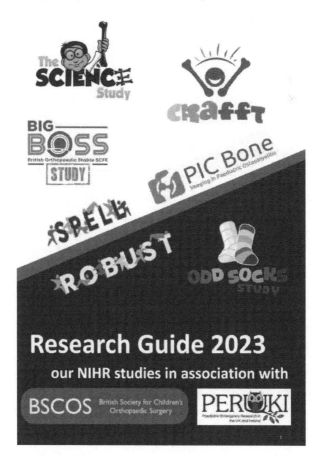

BSCOS – The first 40 years

The Publicity subcommittee

Our most recently formed subcommittee seeks to address challenges in communicating well with our members, with potential future members, with children and their families, and more broadly within society.

For many years we have come to rely on our website, and email, as our primary mode of communication. These modalities continue to serve us well, we rarely resort to licking stamps in any context these days. The work of David Rowland, developer of our website deserves special thanks in this regard. Few of us understand the 'code' that he mastered for us, nor the huge number of hours he spent to enable integrated membership, educational content and interaction on one platform, www.bscos.org.uk. Whilst we will be employing a company to sustain this work in future, the society has benefitted hugely from what he did for us, quietly behind the scenes, over many years.

Recent years have also seen an explosion in the range and immersion of day-to-day life in a much broader range of electronic communication tools. Social media is seemingly a beast that cannot be sated, yet our Society must recognise and respond to the era we live in.

Our publicity subcommittee was formed to lead our society forward in addressing the facebook, instagram, twitter dominated world that our younger members, at least, are familiar with.
Yet the Publicity committee has a broader remit still, leading the way in the pandemic to deliver patient care messaging directly concerning removal of casts at home and avoiding injury. These efforts drew praise from our international partner organisations.

Whether it is attracting future generations of Orthopaedic Surgeons to our subspecialty, promoting materials to the parent/patient population, advocating for children's orthopaedics in the wider public arena, or communicating well with our members, we will rely on our publicity subcommittee to lead us forward.

Short life working groups

Alongside our established subcommittees we have seen a number of short life working groups deliver on specific areas of interest to the Society.

An early venture in this direction concerned the place for Virtual Fracture Clinics, reporting in 2017.

A joint group with BASK has reported on the management of anterior cruciate injuries in the skeletally immature, resulting in a BOAST in 2022. Further work by a similar group concerning patellofemoral joint instability is underway.

Whilst the above could rightly be considered to be delivering consensus, they predated a more formalised Delphi approach (https://en.wikipedia.org/wiki/Delphi_method) in a set of Consensus groups that the Society formed since 2019.
These have reported on the management of Congenital Talipes Equinovarus, on Developmental Hip Dysplasia, and on Musculoskeletal Infection. Further topics that

have now been embarked on include idiopathic toe walking and flat feet.

It seems likely the place for SLWGs remains where a specific and well-defined topic needs our attention.

Significant moments

Alongside the establishment of research, education and publicity subcommittees of the Board, there have been many innovations in our 40-year history that have contributed to make us what we are today.

There follow but a few examples of these significant moments:

Current Concepts Courses

Tony Catterall's legacy goes further than forming BSCOS itself, exemplified in Current Concepts Courses that he began in London, and which now run every third year in cities across the UK. These are ever popular meetings, filled with intense content, bring the latest research to bear in clinical practice targeted to our Consultant membership. Here we see Mr Gargan holding forth in Edinburgh in 2019.

As part of the educational strategy of the Society ahead the future of current concepts will focus around two themes, namely a highly selected update on the latest evidence in a given area and secondly invited experts delivering discussions framed around challenging cases and complications.

Annual meetings

Our Annual Scientific meetings have been a mainstay of BSCOS since its inception. The list of venues and topics and hosts can be seen in the appendix to this volume.

These have formed a backbone to the Society both in educational content, for the opportunity to socialise with colleagues, and to encourage the next generation of paediatric orthopaedic surgeons through their presentation of novel scientific research.

In 2014 the Society moved for the first time from a one to a two-day scientific meeting, hosted in Aberdeen. There was considerable nervousness in the Board at the time – would members come to an extended event? And to the far reaches of northern Scotland at that? Happily, the meeting saw record attendance and notably facilitated a greater opportunity for socialising with a memorable Ceilidh.

Since then, the two-day meeting in the early Spring has become a firm part of  the calendar for paediatric Orthopaedic Surgeons, trainees and affiliated health professionals.

Hosting the event has become ever more complex and in recent years benefits from the support of professional organisers though at its heart the event remains under the ownership of a local team of paediatric orthopaedic surgeons.

BSCOS at the BOA

The Society has for many years sponsored an educational event at BOA annual congresses to bring paediatric orthopaedic educational content to a wider audience.

For our colleagues whose paediatic practice is limited only to trauma, the interest in BSCOS sponsored revalidation sessions at the BOA remains strong. Along with joint sessions run with other sub-specialty societies, in this way, we contribute to the wider education of Orthopaedic surgeons.

Additional content for Specialty trainees is now also offered on the Friday of BOA meetings, aimed at supporting FRCSOrth exam preparation for seniors and as practical skills development opportunity for those in earlier years of training.

Joint Meetings

BSCOS has developed fraternal relations with other national paediatric orthopaedic societies. These include BLRS, BASK, POSNA, POSI, SOFOP, EPOS, APOS, SPOS, and of course the British Orthopaedic Association.

Occasional overseas joint meetings have been popular. Here we see gathered delegates at the combined meeting with SOFOP in Caen in 2009.

Increasing our connections with colleagues overseas is a future aspiration for our society, beginning with collaborative webinars and planned exchanges with our colleagues in the Paediatric Orthopaedic Society of India (POSI).

Affiliate members

From 2015, in response to requests from allied health professionals and in recognition of the growing importance of multidisciplinary team working across the spectrum of paediatric orthopaedic practice, the Society introduced an affiliate membership. The annual meeting of the society has afforded our affiliate members an opportunity to engage with each other through parallel education sessions. We also seek to welcome interested affiliate members to participate in our Society's broader work through our consensus groups and short life working groups.

Early years

Consultants within their first five years of appointment to the grade have been recognised to need our particular support as a Society. Our Board has recently benefitted from the election of an 'Early Years' member.

As a result, from 2023, we now have two annual Gwyn Evans Early Years Fellowships, named in recognition of the late Gwyn Evans' devotion to training, providing support for travelling fellowships across centres in the UK for recently appointed colleagues looking to further develop their skills and experience.

Beyond our shores

The emphasis of BSCOS will ever be orthopaedic surgery in the UK, however, through the initiatives of individual member enthusiasm, we have an increasing awareness of the global unmet needs of children in low- and middle-income countries.

This has been realised in care, often combined with training, provided by our members in diverse locations, through partner organisations such as Mercy Ships, CURE, Global Clubfeet, 'Walk for Life' amongst others.

At our 2023 Annual General Meeting we agreed to support our own first initiative of this kind, on a joint basis with POSNA to provide educational courses in East, Central and Southern Africa through COSECSA, for trainees and Consultants working across sub-Saharan Africa.

Identity

The BSCOS 'logo' was initially a simple representation of the initials each captured on a

blue tile as shown in the Presidential Medal here. The medal was kindly donated to the society in 2010 by one of its founders, Tony Catterall.

Mr Benson's artistic endeavours brought about a teddy bear apparently riding a bone which was immortalised in the ties and scarves of the society.

Whilst this has stood the test of time, bridging from 20th to 21st centuries, in 2013 there was something of a competition to renew the logo. A simple design from Mr Flowers of white and red won out.

Recent enthusiasm for a more child-friendly iteration of our identity did not generate a successful replacement, the membership voting to continue the white and red logo pictured here at Current Concepts 2019 in Edinburgh.

Inclusion and Diversity

Recent years have seen growing awareness of the need to consciously work to deliver an inclusive and diverse environment in Children's Orthopaedics, reflecting similar priorities across society.

In 2018 we commissioned an independent report into inclusion and diversity.

Without exception, interviewees emphasised that BSCOS is a particularly friendly, welcoming society and it was reassuring that the report author could find no evidence of overt discrimination.

Nonetheless, it was recognised that the diversity of the membership of the society could be better represented in its leadership and structures. Happily, this work had already begun, in divesting the Board of its singular responsibility, and the growth of opportunities to become involved in subcommittees, consensus groups and other aspects of the Societies activities.

Through engagement with membership, a reformed constitutional arrangement was introduced. This included a Diversity and Inclusion lead member on the Board. Additionally, a Board member specifically representing those from early years as a consultant, as well as those working in District General Hospital settings were introduced.

The fruits of these changes continue to be realised in initiatives such as the early years fellowship, mentoring and networking groups.

Divisions of labour

'Every undertaker in manufacture finds, that the more he can subdivide the tasks of his workmen, and the more hands he can employ on separate articles, the more are his expenses diminished, and his profits increased.'

Adam Ferguson, Essay on the History of Civil Society, 1767.

Although Adam Smith is broadly credited with the economic enlightenment of the division of labour in his famed description of a pin factory in his work 'The Wealth of Nations', his less well known Scottish contemporary Adam Ferguson pre-empted him by a full ten years!

We have all witnessed an unfolding reality whereby a subdivision of labour has become manifest across Medicine as a whole and no less Orthopaedics as a discipline.

There has been a presumption of benefit from greater focus of skill in a narrower field of practice. Specialisation has given way to 'sub' specialisation with gathering pace in the latter half of the 20th and early part of the 21st Century. Paediatric orthopaedics itself as a discipline is of course an example thereof.

The drivers for this trend are multiple and include the desire to gather together expertise and experience in uncommon conditions and procedural skills to deliver more consistent and, it is hoped, improved outcomes. The advent of revalidation in Medicine and an enhanced scrutiny of outcomes inevitably discourages the experimental and occasional practitioner. Yet the influence of other spheres of practice has also been significant. The risk management safety-based decision by anaesthetic colleagues to restrict infant anaesthetic provision at smaller centres in the early 2000s severely curtailed surgical practice in younger children and drove early surgical interventions into larger hospital settings.

The story of subdivision is not over. Within children's orthopaedics we in turn have not been immune to this trend. The advent of subspecialty super-specialisation is upon us; recent years have seen some colleagues focussing on a narrowing area of subspecialty practice: upon conditions such as Cerebral Palsy, Developmental Dysplasia of the Hip and Clubfoot. The place for a generalist paediatric orthopod is currently secure, though the future may reflect further development along this trajectory, particularly if outcome data further supports the idea that volume drives quality.

The recent GIRFT work led by James Hunter asks legitimate and searching questions about unjustifiable variations in practice across the country, and the wisdom of individual practitioners caring for a tiny number of  children with complex presenting pathology. Where outcomes are poorer this is a legitimate driver for further change.

The tension between provision local to the patient, which can be clearly justified for something like common fractures, and at a centre with the numbers to drive experience and provide evidence of quality for less frequent conditions; is ongoing and not an easy circle to square.

Perhaps the most obvious manifestation of our own desire for subdivision of labour is in our sub-specialty groups, some more established than others, but each with self-selected memberships of the interested and committed:

BSSCP

The British Society for Surgery in Cerebral Palsy draws together Surgeons (and more recently some allied health professionals) with a particular interest in musculoskeletal aspects of Cerebral Palsy. It had its origins, like BSCOS itself, in a friendly grouping of those who sought to share learning and seek collegial expertise for challenging cases. The attractiveness of honest and open discourse has caused this 'CP club' which still eschews formality to grow and grow and attract a number of colleagues from across Europe to its annual meetings which combine presentation of member led scientific papers and case discussion with a healthy dose of social interaction.

Previous meetings have ranged across the UK and Europe (including Aschau im Cheimgau, Berlin and Rummelsberg), with occasional visits further afield, notably in 2013 to visit Freeman Miller in Delaware.

The Nemours Delaware trip of 2013.

Michael Wachowsky hosts the 2019 meeting
in Rummelsberg

There is no shortage of ongoing enthusiasm for this model of learning. After the hiatus of the pandemic in 2021, fifty members of the club gathered to consider surgical interventions, gait analysis, case discussion and relevant research.

The CP club in action... Aberdeen 2021

UKCCG

The United Kingdom Clubfoot Consensus Group draws together surgeons alongside allied health professionals with an interest in the condition, and most particularly in promoting the Ponseti method of treatment as best practice in the treatment of congenital talipes equinovarus.

The group was established by a core team of UK clinicians championed by Naomi Davis with invaluable support from the late Fred Dietz (Iowa) and has sought to promote consistently high standards of practice in the management of clubfoot in the UK by promoting regional networking, information sharing and a programme of hands-on training events provided in association with the *Global Clubfoot Initiative* for which there is sustained demand.

Standards for treating idiopathic clubfoot by the Ponseti method were agreed by the core team in 2011 and were taken forward at the 1st European Clubfoot Consensus Group who met in July 2012 and were published in 2013 (J Child Orthop ISSN 1863-2521).

Working alongside The Global Clubfoot Initiative a two-level training programme for the Ponseti method has been adapted and adopted into UK practice, ensuring a consistent understanding of the technique.

Whilst Ponseti has 'solved' the vast majority of clubfeet, International Clubfoot Conferences have been organised to explore answers to the ongoing issues raised by feet that simply will not behave.

DDH groups

Whilst less formally constituted to date, regional groups of surgeons with an interest in Developmental Dysplasia of the Hip are actively exploring the screening conundrums in DDH and collaborating on optimising treatment.

Recent consensus group work on this condition highlighted areas of ongoing uncertainty that will undoubtedly benefit from active research in coming years.

Progress

'Every day you may make progress. Every step may be fruitful. Yet there will stretch out before you an ever-lengthening, ever-ascending, ever-improving path. You know you will never get to the end of the journey. But this, so far from discouraging, only adds to the joy and glory of the climb.'

Winston S. Churchill

Forty years have seen significant change in the Orthopaedic care of children. None more so than in the case of Congenital Talipes Equinovarus, or Clubfoot which is surely an exemplar of transformation of care through application of sound scientific method in our subspecialty.

Treatments including the brutality of the Thomas wrench had already been replaced by soft tissue surgeries, most commonly the postero-medial release. These and other historical forms of management had overall restoration of foot shape in common but with costly compromise to the underlying structural integrity of the foot. Form was restored over and above function with chronic pain being the hallmark legacy of a legion of described surgical interventions.

Ignacio Ponseti brought meticulous and vigorous scientific method to bear on the problem of clubfoot. His crucial observation that the talar head forms the logical fulcrum around which correction of a clubfoot  could be achieved, has transformed care of infants born with this condition. Although first published in 1980, disappointingly it took some twenty years for the gradual corrective serial casting treatment devised by Ponseti to filter into widespread practice in the UK. The prospect of supple, pain free feet in almost all cases was eventually and irresistibly persuasive. Over time the previous standard of surgical release has been reduced to the occasional, the resistant and the desperate.

Ponseti's story must surely be one of the most significant and notable transformations in paediatric orthopaedic care since the advent of antibiotics, and in turn safe anaesthesia before that.

The story is all the more remarkable for it is a treatment that can and has been effectively adopted in diverse worldwide economic situations restoring functional feet in Bangladesh and Malawi with equal impact alongside London and Boston.

In contrast to the settled primacy of Ponseti's technique for clubfeet, there remain other conditions that are significantly challenging evidenced by multiple treatment options. Optimal management for some continues to be mired in variable depths of uncertainty.

It is perhaps fair to recognise that a coordinated focus on rigorous scientific method in paediatric orthopaedics was somewhat piecemeal throughout the history of BSCOS, until the early 2000s, when several stars aligned. Tim Theologis, our President at the time, with great vision, instigated a process to prioritise research goals in partnership with the James Lind Alliance. This work unlocked significant national funding that has enabled properly resourced and well powered studies of paediatric orthopaedic conditions to be undertaken on a coordinated national basis, spearheaded by the indubitably *Awesome* Dan Perry in Liverpool. Perthes Disease, Slipped Upper Femoral Epiphysis, Multilevel surgery in cerebral palsy, Distal Radial fractures and Medial Epicondyle fractures of the Elbow have been early targets for rigorous study. More are promised.

Alongside such exciting developments in original research we have also benefitted from systematic and enhanced scrutiny of current practice. This came to fruition in 2022 when BSCOS welcomed James Hunter's 'Getting it right first time' (GIRFT) report on paediatric orthopaedic services in England. It shed light on, and brought challenges to the variations and anachronisms of children's orthopaedic care that only a broad bird's eye view of our current services could identify.

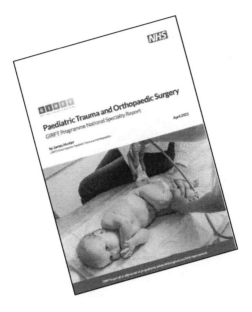

It is this report, its recommendations, and our response to them as children's orthopaedic surgeons that rightly sets the framework for future work of our society and its members as we look forward from 40 years of growth to the next chapter.

Regional variations

A number of groups have operated informally and locally across the UK.

In North East England, **NEPOG** (NE Paediatric Orthopaedic Group) meets 2-3 x per year for case presentations, discussion, and a meal.

Keith Tucker established the **East Anglian paediatric group** meetings, based mainly on the original BSCOS meeting format and he notes that in early years they always invited a 'big shot' from BSCOS to sit in and offer opinion.

In Scotland, **SPOC** (Scottish Paediatric Orthopaedic Club) was formed to bring together colleagues working in Paediatric Orthopaedic surgery from across Scotland to an annual meeting in Perth with case discussion and audit presentations followed by dinner at a local hostelry. More recently this has increased to a biannual meeting. The principal players in the early years in Scotland were David Sherlock from Glasgow, Malcolm Macnicol from

Edinburgh, and Alistair Swanson. Mirroring but organisationally lagging BSCOS, SPOC has grown from a friendly handful of enthusiasts to a larger group of clinicians and following a combined meeting with the Swedish Paediatric Orthopaedic Society was in recent years responsible for successfully introducing the Cerebral Palsy surveillance programme 'CPIPS' to Scotland, a first for the UK, led by James Robb with the support of Gunner Hagglund (Sweden). This programme has been subsequently adopted more widely across the UK.

The original CPIPS team included James Robb & Mark Gaston (Edinburgh), Heather Read (Glasgow), Jamie Maclean & Donald Campbell (Dundee), Simon Barker (Aberdeen), Peter Donnelly (Professor of Public Health in St Andrews), and Madeleine Baines (MRes student 2010-11).

James Robb comments that he thought *it was important that we understood CP referral patterns, transition and how the Swedish CPUP model would work in Scotland before introducing CPIPS in 2013.* Two further MRes

Students were key: Kimberley Stevenson (2011-12), a Fulbright Scholar from the US, researched the applicability of the CPUP model to Scotland and then Alice Wright (2011-12) investigated transition from paediatric to adult services for children with CP.

The original CPIPS team at a meeting in Perth.

'Rogues gallery'

Dinners have ever been part of the BSCOS experience and a fulsome expression of the friendliness of the Society.

After dinner speeches have been of mixed pedigree. Few can forget the memorable and encouraging talk from the celebrated author Bill Bryson at our meeting in Leicester in 2013. He had us spellbound and gave a ringing endorsement to our profession's efforts to bring the very best of care to our patients in the face of a cynical world. Memorable in a different way was the Liverpool dinner of 2015. Mr Bruce's look of horror was priceless as a local tour guide who at first effused a sense of grandfatherly benevolence gradually, incongruously, and inexplicably descended into ever more bawdy humour. It has perhaps been a wise move towards brevity in our dinner speeches in subsequent years.

There follow a small sample of the many images from conferences past...

Appendices

Past Annual Meetings

Year	Location	Topics	Host
2023	Southampton	Neuromuscular	C Edwards
2022	Tunbridge Wells	Upper Limb	M Katchaburian
2021	Online – due to pandemic	Major Trauma	BSCOS Board
2020	Cancelled – due to pandemic	-	-
2019	Norwich	Deformity: Science & Surgery	A Sanghrajka
2018	Stoke on Trent	Trauma, Paediatric Knee	D Emery
2017	Glasgow	Adolescent hip Combined SBOF meeting (Swedish)	D Rowland
2016	Stoke Mandeville	Spinal injury, Orthotics, Networks	J Hicks
2015	Liverpool	CP, Spine	C Bruce
2014	Aberdeen	Controversies	S Barker
2013	July – Leicester Jan – St Georges	Skeletal dysplasias Prenatal diagnosis	A Abraham K Daly
2012	July – Plymouth Jan – Belfast	Trauma Perthes	R Jeffrey A Cosgrove
2011	Jun – Oxford Jan – Sheffield	'Beyond Britain' Combined with BLRS	A Wainwright J Fernandes
2010	Jun – Stanmore Jan – Coventry	Upper Limb DDH	S Tennant G Pattison
2009	Jun – Caen (FR) Jan – Birmingham	Combined SOFOP meeting Adolescent/Young Adult Hip	- J O'Hara

BSCOS – The first 40 years

2008	Jun – Bristol	Perthes	G Atherton
	Jan - Taunton	NAI	C Ogilvie
2007	Jun – Glasgow	Infection	R Duncan
	Jan – Newcastle	Neuromuscular	P Henman
2006	Jun – Blackburn	Perthes	R Paton
	Jan – Milton Keynes	Injury prevention	G Miller
2005	Jun – Dublin		M Stevens
	Jan – Barts & The London	Trauma	M Barry
2004	Jun – Edinburgh	Combined with	J Robb
	Jan – Leicester	GEOP	C Kershaw
2003	Jun – Sheffield	Metabolic Bone	M Bell
	Jan – Bristol	Disease	M Gargan
2002	Jun – Toulouse (Fr)	Combined with GEOP	
	Jan – Southampton	Fractures	N Clarke
2001	Jun – Oswestry	Neuromuscular	G Evans
	Jan – Milton Keynes	Playground injuries	
2000	Jun – Leeds	Combined with	B Scott
	Jan – London	GEOP	D Hunt
1999	Jul – Edinburgh	Tumours	J Robb
	Jan – Nottingham	Trauma	J Hunter
1998	Jul – Liverpool	Muscular Dystrophy	J Dorgan
	Jan – Swansea	Growth plate	D Jones
1997	Jul – Middlesborough	Technical advances	R Montgomery
	Jan – Birmingham	CTEV	C Bradish
1996	Jul – Oxford	Skeletal Dysplasias	M Benson
	Jan – St Mary's	Infection	D Hunt
1995	Jul – Cancelled – due to rail strike	-	-
	Jan – Southampton	Trauma	N Clarke
1994	Jul – Canterbury	Cerebral Palsy	M Conybeare
	Jan – Sheffield	Leg lengthening	M Bell

116

BSCOS – The first 40 years

1993	Jul – Dublin	DDH in older child	T O'Brien
	Jan – Manchester	Cerebral Palsy	C Galasko
1992	Jul – Glasgow	The foot	G Bennet
	Jan – London	Neuromuscular	B Roper
1991	Jul – Newcastle	Infection	M Leonard
	Jan – Stoke	Forearm fractures	D Edwards
1990	Jul – Edinburgh	Late hip problems	M Macnicol
	Jan – Norwich	CTEV	K Tucker
1989	Jul – Oswestry	Skeletal dysplasia	G Evans
	Jan – Cardiff	DDH	B McKibbon
1988	Jul – Westminster	Leg lengthening	P Aichroth
	Jan – Bristol	Cerebral Palsy	P Witherow
1987	Jul – Southampton	DDH	J Wilkinson
		DDH	M Benson
	Jan – Oxford		
1986	Jul – Liverpool	DDH	R Owen
	Jan – Birmingham	Spine dislocation	M Harrison
1985	Jul – Nottingham	NAI	C Colton
	Jan – Gt Ormond St	Perthes	J Fixsen
1984	Charing Cross Hospital	The foot	J Sharrard

Recipients of the Sharrard Medal

The Society Medal is presented on the award of Honorary Membership of the Society, and for significant contributions to the Society and to Children's Orthopaedics since 2006.

Mr Catterall, in his acceptance speech compared his experience of BSCOS to being a parent, first of a helpless infant, then an unruly teenager, and finally (perhaps) a mature adult.

Sadly, a full list has not been retained in our Society Archives however some of the past recipients of the medal include:

2006	J Fixsen A Catterall T O'Brien (Dublin)
2013	G Bennet M Bell
2015	J Robb
2018	T Slongo M Askenberger D Sherlock
2019	K Tucker
2022	D Hunt P Armstrong (USA)
2023	G Evans
2024	J Maclean J Wright (Canada)

Peter Armstrong, a friend of BSCOS over many years, is awarded the first International Honorary Membership of the Society in 2022.

Past Presidents of the Society

2020-2022	Colin Bruce
2018-2020	Tim Theologis
2016-2018	Mark Flowers
2014-2016	Aresh Hashemi Najid
2012-2014	James Robb
2010-2012	James Hunter
2008-2010	Chris Bradish
2006-2008	Nick Clarke
2004-2006	David Hunt
2002-2004	Mike Bell
2000-2002	George Bennet
1998-2000	Gwyn Evans
1996-1998	Mike Benson
1994-1996	Tony Caterall
1992-1994	Tony Caterall
1990-1992	John Sharrard
1988-1990	John Sharrard
1986-1988	John Fixsen
1984-1986	John Fixsen

Roll of Current Members of the Society

Members of the British Society of Children's Orthopaedic Surgery in good standing at the time of going to press are included here:

Ordinary 227

A Alexander Aarvold, Alwyn Abraham, Akinwande Adedapo, Oluwarantimi Adoyele, Arash Afsharpad, Mubashshar Ahmad, James Aird, Farhan Ali, Farhan Alvi, Suresh Annamalai, Elizabeth Ashby, Rajan Asirvatham, W Guy Atherton, Koldo Azurza,

B Edward Bache, David Baker, Emily Baird, James Ballard, Simon Barker, James Barnes, Matthew Barry, Alf Bass, Simon Bennett, Caroline Blakey, Jose Blanco, Anna Bridgens, James Brousil, Colin Bruce, Helen Bryant, Rachel Buckingham, Vittoria Bucknall, Pranai Buddhdev, Kate Bugler,

C Peter Calder, Donald Campbell, Graeme Carlile, Clare Carpenter, M Belen Carsi, John Cashman, Helen Chase, Mariusz Chomicki, Qaisar Choudry, Anna Clarke, Nicholas Clarke, Christopher Coates, Stephen Cooke, David Conlan, Aidan Cosgrove, Thomas Crompton,

D Jo Dartnell, Naomi Davis, John Davies, Nev Davies, Gavin de Kiewiet, Laura Deriu, Richard Dodds, Sara Dorman, Tim Dougall, Catherine Duffy, Jonathan Dwyer,

E Deborah Eastwood, Philip Edge, Caroline Edwards, Amr Elkhouly, Kirsten Elliott, David Emery, Owain Evans, Stuart Evans,

F James Fagg, David Ferguson, Kim Ferguson, James Fernandes, Gregory Firth, Julian Flynn, Robert Freeman, Andrew Furlong, Adelle Fishlock, Mark Flowers, Anne Foster, Paddy Foster,

G Andrew Gaffey, Sangeet Gangadharan, Neeraj Garg, Martin Gargan, Mark Gaston, Caroline Geddes, Yael Gelfer, Paul Gibbons, Stephen Giles, Nick Green,

H Mohamed Hafez, Aresh Hashemi-Nejad, Amanda Hawkins, Russell Hawkins, Annabel Hayward, Sandeep Hemmadi, John Henderson, Philip Henman, Jo Hicks, Chris Hill, Sally Hobson, David Hollinghurst, Ben Holroyd, Colin Holton, Richard Hopcroft, Alison Hulme, James Hunter, Rachel Hutchinson,

I,J,K Sarah Irby, Azal Jagaonkar, Kyle James, Leroy James, Lisa Jeavons, Robert Jeffery, Verne Johnson, Sujit Kadambande, Marcos Katchburian, Sarmad Kazzaz, Nigel Keily, Tahir Khan, Michail Kokkinakis, Alpesh Kothari, Dominique Knight, Robert Kucharski, Sanjay Kumar,

L,M Om Lahoti, Mark Latimer, Linghong Lee, Ed Lindisfarne, Sanjeev Madan, Claudia Maizen, Dimitrios Manoukian, Subramanyam Maripuri, Andrew McBride, Janet McCaul, Anthony McEvoy, James McKenzie, Juergen Messner, James Metcalfe, Max Mifsud, Piers Mitchell, Leanora Mills, Neel Mohan, Fergal Monsell, Manolis Morakis, Elizabeth Moulder, Emily Mounsey, Claire Murnaghan, Alistair Murray, Kom Muthusamy,

123

N,O Ramanathan Natarajan, Stephen Ng Man Sun, Nicolas Nicolaou, Fabian Norman-Taylor, Declan O'Docherty,

P,Q Jonathan Page, Robin Paton, Giles Pattison, Felicity Pease, Anna Peek, Daniel Perry, Nick Peterson, James Phillips, Sarah Phillips, Virginie Pollet, Hari Prem, Kathryn Price, Neil Price, Chris Prior, Assad Qureshi,

R Darius Rad, Rohan Rajan, Heather Read, Daniel Reed, Andreas Rehm, Michael Reidy, Robert Richards, Elaine Robinson, Andreas Roposch, David Rowland,

S Mohamed Sabouni, Anish Sanghrajka, Khaled Sarraf, Olivia Malaga Shaw, Rachel Short, Srinivasan Shyamsundar, Shabih Siddiqui, Alex Smith, Innes Smith, Thomas Southorn, Veronique Spiteri, Kuldeep Stohr, Sean Symons,

T Suhayl Tafazal, Christopher Talbot, Rebecca Tate, Colm Taylor, Sally Tennant, Tim Theologis, Joanna Thomas, Simon Thomas, Madhu Tiruveedhula, Aureola Tong, Nirmal Tulwa, Jim Turner,

U,V Michael Uglow, Ram Vadivelu, Themistoklis Vampertzis, Bobin Varghese, Krishna Vemulapalli,

W Farokh Wadia, Andrew Wainwright, Roger Walton, Guy Wansbrough, Kakra Wartemberg, Dan Westacott, Sam Weston-Simons, James Widnall, Breanna Winger, Derfel Williams, Paul Williams, David Wright, Jonathan Wright,

Y,Z Andea Yeo, Marcin Zgoda.

BSCOS – The first 40 years

Honorary 12
Mike Bell, George Bennet, Michael Benson, Anthony Caterall, John Clegg, David Jones, Jamie Maclean, Malcolm Macnicol, James Robb, David Sherlock, Keith Tucker, John Wilkinson.

Retired 35
Allen Baker, Carol Brignall, Richard Buxton, Nicholas Clarke, Mark Cornell, Harry Cowie, Karen Daly, Geraint Davies, John Day, John Dorgan, Roderick Duncan, David Jameson Evans, Lawrence Freedman, Charles Galasko, David Hunt, Thampy Jacob, Andrew Jackson, Cledwyn Jones, Christopher Kershaw, Mike Laverick, Paul Marshall, Alan Moulton, Andrew Murray, Judy Murray, John Nixon, Colin Ogilvie, David Riley, Guy Rooker, Douglas Sammon, Tim Stahl, Michael Stephens, Tudor Thomas, Irene van der Ploeg, Neil Wilson.

Overseas 5
Sattar Alshryda, Anand Gorva, Jean Marc Guichet, Ibrar Majid, Jaap Tolk.

Honorary Overseas 3
Peter Armstrong, Kerr Graham, Jim Wright

Associate 61
Ady Abdelhaq, Usman Abdulkadir, Mohammed Al-Ashqar, Mutasem Aldhoon, John Amen, Anouska Ayub, Sheba Zulaikha Basheer, Luckshman Bavan, Ian Baxter, Becky

Beamish, Stephanie Buchan, Charlotte Carpenter, Benjamin Chatterton, Richard Connell, Joanna Craven, Rebecca Critchley, Jennifer Dunn, Khaled Elawady, Munzir Gaboura, Nikos Giannakakis, Catherine Gilliland, Ehab Girgis, Nitish Gogi, Zakir Haider, Taushaba Hossain, Katie Hughes, Simon Humphry, Walid Hussein, Richard Hutchinson, John Jeffery, Akib Khan, Sayeed Khan, Binu Kurian, Tariq Kwaees, Alison Liddle, Ben Marson, Ellen Martin, Gregory McConaghie, Hannah Meacher, Rajiv Merchant, Hussein Noureddine, Ignatius Lew, Pinelopi Linardatou Novak, Mohamed Osman, Anbuchezhian Palanivel, Chang Park, Deepika Pinto, Ben Rand, Patrick Reynolds, Anna Rieman, Neil Segaran, Ewan Semple, Gaurangkumar Shah, Ishani Shah, Robert Silverwood, Francis Sim, Abhinav Singh, Gillian Smith, Chun Tang, Laura Tillotson, Mughees Zafar

Affiliate (AHPs) 40

Lisa Armour, Victoria Brattan, Hayley Briscoe, Rachel Bye, Alice Castle, Sarah Dewhurst, Sam Double, Christine Douglas, Mia Dunkley, Vicky Easton, Adam Galloway, Alex Gill, Leigh Hailstone, Debbie Hall, Jennifer Harris, Katie Hayes, Danielle Hewish, Sarah Hill, Bethan Hinchey, Annie Hurley, Julia Judd, Angie Lee, Lucy Llewellyn-Stanton, Katie Lowe, Charlotte Martin, Stacey Maughan, Kerry McGarrity, Anna Mcnee, Sarah Paterson, Angela Riddle, Aisling Russell, Fran Sutton, Helen Swain, Amanda Trees, Rebecca Tunbridge, Craig Walsh, Denise Watson-Tann, Michelle Wood, David Wormald, Elizabeth Wright.

Medical Student 4

Sebastian Barclay, Aaron Gan, Lucas Ho, Josiah Joseph

Total roll of BSCOS = 387 members

Geography of the Society

Members of BSCOS truly cover the whole of the United Kingdom in provision of children's orthopaedic and trauma care at over 75 centres across the country. Details below are self-reported locations of ordinary members in good standing [correct at Summer 2023].

The South West

Bristol Royal Hospital for Children
Martin Gargan
Anna Clarke
Dominique Knight
Fergal Monsell
James Barnes
Guy Atherton
Simon Thomas
Andrew McBride
Jim Turner

Cornwall
Russell Hawkins

Royal Devon & Exeter
Laura Tillotson

Royal United Hospital, Bath
James Fagg

Swindon & Marlborough
Sarah Irby
David Hollinghurst

Taunton

Emily Mounsey

Torbay

Guy Wansborough

The South & South East

Basildon & Thurrock
Madhu Tiruveedhula

Bedford Hospitals
Philip Edge

Brighton & Sussex University Hospitals
Subramanyam Maripuri
Thomas Crompton
Kyle James

Buckinghamshire Health (Stoke Mandeville)
Joanna Hicks

Chelsea & Westminster
Stuart Evans
Alison Hulme
Stephen Ng Man Sun

Evelina Children's (Guys & St Thomas')
Martin Kokkinakis
Sam Weston-Simons
Daniel Reed

Frimley Park
Azal Jalgaonkar
Sarmad Kazzaz

Great Ormond St (London)
Deborah Eastwood
Fabian Norman Taylor
Andreas Roposch

Kings's College Hospital
Om Lahoti
Sarah Phillips

Maidstone & Tunbridge Wells
Marcos Katchburian
Jo Dartnell
Adoyele Oluwarantimi

Mid & South Essex (Southend)
Sean Symons
Kakra Wartemberg

Northampton General
Ramanathan Natarajan
Kom Muthusamy

Milton Keynes
Julian Flynn

Oxford University Hospitals
Rachel Buckingham
Timolean Theologis
Andrew Wainwright
Max Mifsud
Alpesh Kothari

Plymouth Hospitals
Robert Jeffery
Ben Holroyd
James Aird
James Metcalfe

Portsmouth Hospitals
Robert Richards

Queens Hospital, Romford
Krishna Vemulapalli

Royal Berks & Battle (Reading)
Richard Dodds
Nev Davies
Amr Elkhouly

Royal Free London
Olivia Malaga Shaw

Royal London Hospital
Claudia Maizen
Dimitrios Manoukian
Gregory Firth
Themistoklis Vampertzis

Royal National Orthopaedic (Stanmore)
Aresh Hashemi Nejad
Peter Calder
Sally Tennant
Jonathan Wright
Tahir Khan
Deborah Eastwood

Royal Surrey (Guildford)
Christopher Coates

Southampton
Alexander Aarvold
Farokh Wadia
Kirsten Elliot
Caroline Edwards

Matthew Barry
Ed Lindisfarne
Darius Rad
Simon Bennet
Mike Uglow

St George's
Yael Gelfer
Neel Mohan
Anna Bridgens
Andrea Yeo

St Mary's
Khaled Sarraf

East Anglia

Cambridge
Mark Latimer
Andreas Rehm
Kuldeep Stohr
Pranai Buddhev
David Conlan
Elizabeth Ashby

Norfolk & Norwich
Rachael Hutchinson
Anish Sanghrajka
Helen Chase
Sangeet Gangadharan

Peterborough
Piers Mitchell
Jose Blanco
Mariusz Chomicki

Suffolk
Graeme Carlile

The Midlands

Birmingham Children's
Andrew Gaffey
Edward Bache
James Phillips
Hari Prem
Joanna Thomas
Ram Vadivelu
Veronique Spiteri

Coventry & Warwickshire
Stephen Cooke
Giles Pattison
Daniel Westacott
Chris Hill

Derby
Rohan Rajan
Suhayl Tafazal
James Brousil

Kettering General Hospital
Srinivasan Shyamsundar
Shabih Siddiqui

Nottingham University Hospitals
James Hunter
Kathryn Price
David Bryson

Robert Jones & Agnes Hunt (Oswestry)
Nigel Kiely
Robert Freeman
Andrew Roberts
Derfel Williams

Royal Orthopaedic Hospital (Birmingham)
James McKenzie

United Lincolnshire
Rajan Asirvatham
Thomas Southorn

University Hospitals Leicester
Andrew Furlong
Alwyn Abraham
Anna Peek
Assad Qureshi
Suresh Annamalai

University Hosp North Mids (Stoke on Trent)
Jonathan Dwyer
Emma Shears
David Emery
Maria Carsi

Wolverhampton
Bobin Varghese

Gloucester
Sanjay Kumar

The North West

Lancashire Teaching Hospitals
Anthony McEvoy

Morecambe Bay Hospitals
Paul Marshall

North Cumbria (Carlisle)
Lisa Jeavons

Royal Blackburn
Qaisar Choudry
Robin Paton
Sunil D'Souza

Royal Liverpool Childrens (Alder Hey)
Alf Bass
Colin Bruce
Daniel Perry
David Wright
Neeraj Garg
Leroy James
Christopher Talbot
Vittoria Bucknall
Chris Prior

Nick Peterson
Roger Walton
James Widnall

Royal Manchester Children's

Naomi Davis
Anne Foster
Manolis Morakis
Virginie Pollet
Ali Farhan

BMI Beaumont (Bolton)

John Henderson

The North East, Yorks & Humberside

Hull & East Yorks
Verne Johnson
Sally Hobson
Elizabeth Moulder

James Cook (South Tees)
Richard Hopcroft
Akinwande Adedapo
Rebecca Tate
David Ferguson

Leeds Teaching
Colin Holton
Paddy Foster
Mohamed Sabouni
Adele Fishlock
Laura Deriu
John Davies
Elaine Robinson

Mid Yorkshire Hospitals (Wakefield)
Nirmal Tulwa
Helen Bryant

Newcastle upon Tyne
Philip Henman

Sheffield
Mark Flowers
James Fernandes
Owain Evans
John Cashman
Sanjeev Madan
Nicolas Nicolaou
Mohamed Hafez
Caroline Blakey
Stephen Giles
Nick Green
Sara Dorman

Sunderland
Gavin de Kiewiet
Ling Hong

University Hospital of North Durham
Jonathan Page
Mubashshar Ahmad

Doncaster Royal Infirmary
Robert Kucharski

Scotland – Borders

Dumfries & Galloway
Amanda Hawkins

Scotland – Central

Royal Hosp. for Children (Edinburgh)
Juergen Messner
Mark Gaston
Emily Baird
Kate Bugler
Alastair Murray

Royal Hosp. for Children (Glasgow)
David Rowland
Janet McCaul
Alex Smith
Clare Murnaghan
Kim Ferguson
Innes Smith

Crosshouse (Kilmarnock)
Rachel Short
Marcin Zgoda

East Lanarkshire
Annabel Hayward

Scotland – North

Royal Aberdeen Children's
Simon Barker
Leanora Mills
Mike Reidy
Felicity Pease
Tim Dougall

NHS Tayside (Dundee & Perth)
Donald Campbell

Wales

Cardiff & Vale
Clare Carpenter
Sandeep Hemmadi
Declan O'Doherty

Glan Clwyd
Farhan Alvi

Royal Gwent
Sujit Kadambande
David Baker

Morriston Hospital (Swansea)
Neil Price
Paul Williams

Ysbyty Gwynedd, Bangor
Koldo Azurza

Royal Glamorgan
Aureola Tong

Northern Ireland

Royal Belfast Hospital for Sick Children
Aidan Cosgrove
Catherine Duffy
James Ballard

Republic of Ireland

Cork
Colm Taylor

Rules & Byelaws of the Society

The rules of our Society have undergone several iterations as we have grown and developed. A significant change came about with registration as a company in 2013. We are registered in Scotland by quirk of fate rather than design. James Robb who is based in Edinburgh, was president at the time, and put in a huge amount of work to bring about this development.

CERTIFICATE OF INCORPORATION
OF A
PRIVATE LIMITED COMPANY

Company Number **465033**

The Registrar of Companies for Scotland, hereby certifies that

BRITISH SOCIETY FOR CHILDREN'S ORTHOPAEDIC
SURGERY

is this day incorporated under the Companies Act 2006 as a private company, that the
company is limited by guarantee, and the situation of its registered office is in
Scotland.

Given at Companies House, Edinburgh, on **3rd December 2013**.

The above information was communicated by electronic means and authenticated by the
Registrar of Companies under section 1115 of the Companies Act 2006

Companies House

THE OFFICIAL SEAL OF THE
REGISTRAR OF COMPANIES

Members of our Board are governed by the
requirements placed upon Directors of a
Company set out by Companies House, and
particularly by the Company Rules.

We have seen a gradual increase in the size of
the Board to reflect the growing scope of its
activities and a desire to address issues of
diversity and inclusion in recent years.

With the advent of subcommittees and working groups, a number of byelaws have been introduced by the Board to clarify expectations and roles within the Society.

There follows the Company Rules and Society Byelaws as at 2022.

BSCOS Members' Guide

including

Company Rules

and

Society Byelaws

V 2.6

Introduction

The British Society for Children's Orthopaedic Surgery was founded in 1984 to promote Paediatric Orthopaedic Surgery in the UK. The society provides a forum for discussion, promotes research, education, advances in clinical practice and the results of surgical procedures pertaining to the practice of children's orthopaedics and trauma. In 2021 the Society adopted the mission statement: -

"BSCOS supports and promotes the delivery and dissemination of high-quality children's orthopaedic care, education and research."

Membership is open to UK practitioners for whom Children's Orthopaedics represents a substantial part of their practice and professional interest.

BSCOS actively seeks to uphold the principles of equality and diversity in all its activities. We seek to promote an inclusive practice and culture. Membership of the Society brings with it an expectation that these principles will be supported. This applies to all activities of the society.

The Society meets once a year for a scientific meeting involving lectures and papers, and contributes to instructional sessions at the annual British Orthopaedic Association Congress.

BSCOS has alliances with the British Orthopaedic Association (BOA), The European Paediatric Orthopaedic Society (EPOS) and the Paediatric Orthopaedic Society of North America (POSNA), the Australian Paediatric Orthopaedic Society (APOS) and the Paediatric Orthopaedic Society of India (POSI).

This guide is aimed particularly at new members. We hope it helps you to understand your Society and encourages you to get involved. There are lots of opportunities to do so – please take a moment to read about them in the following pages.

BSCOS is known to be a friendly and welcoming Society. We very much hope you experience this! If you have comments and suggestions concerning the Society, please do bring them to the attention of the Board.

Contact us!

Please contact us as follows:

President@bscos.org.uk – to contact the President

Secretary@bscoc.org.uk – for membership queries, GDPR

Treasurer@bscos.org.uk – for expense claim queries, subscription payment queries

Webadmin@bscos.org.uk – for web content

Education@bscos.org.uk – for Educational subcommittee queries

Research@bscos.org.uk – for Research subcommittee queries

DI@bscos.org.uk – for issues relating to equality, diversity & inclusion.

DGH@bscos.org.uk - for issues related to working in non-tertiary/paediatric centres

EY@bscos.org.uk – for issues related to early years working

Membership

The benefits of BSCOS membership include:
- 'Members only' website content
- Favourable rates for meetings
- Access to reciprocal rates for allied society meetings
- Opportunities to serve on Society committees and apply for bursaries
- The chance to participate in, and shape the future of our society

Ordinary membership

Consultant Orthopaedic Surgeons who hold a substantive appointment with a significant paediatric practice are eligible for ordinary membership when supported by two referees of members in good standing.

Ordinary members have a vote at Society meetings and may stand for Board positions as well as subcommittee positions.

Associate membership

This category of membership is open to:

- *Consultant Surgeons from other disciplines and those with locum Consultant Orthopaedic posts who commit a proportion of their clinical time to the management of musculoskeletal conditions in children.
- *Staff, Associate Specialist & Specialty (SAS) Doctors who commit a proportion of their clinical time to the management of children with conditions that result in

regular work alongside children's orthopaedic surgeons.

- Trainees in orthopaedic surgery in possession of a national training number
- Doctors on the specialist register for trauma and orthopaedics practising as Fellows in children's orthopaedic surgery.

*[Consultant and SAS doctor Associate Members may stand for election to subcommittees and working groups of the Society but may not chair subcommittees. They may also attend, but not vote at, the AGM of the Society].

Affiliate membership

Allied health professionals who regularly treat children in an orthopaedic capacity, surgical or otherwise may be considered for affiliate membership. It is expected that this aspect of their work is carried out in conjunction with Ordinary Members of the Society and two references from Ordinary members in good standing are required.

Affiliate members may stand for election to consensus/working groups and subcommittees of the Society but are not eligible to chair these groups nor to stand for the Board.

Overseas membership

This category is appropriate to those Ordinary members who are working abroad.

The Board has discretion to waive fees on application to the Treasurer by those working on an entirely charitable basis in low- and middle-income countries.

Overseas members have a vote in Society elections alongside Ordinary Members. Overseas members may stand for election to Consensus/working groups and subcommittees of the Society provided they can commit to participate fully in the business of the relevant group.

Medical student membership

This category of membership is available at the discretion of the Board for motivated medical students studying in a UK Medical School. It is expected that they would have formed a strong interest in children's orthopaedic surgery during their undergraduate training and have two references from Ordinary members in good standing.

Medical student members are not eligible for subcommittee nor Board membership. They are eligible to attend and present at medical student meetings of the Society.

Subscriptions

The Board sets subscriptions for its membership categories at the Annual meeting of the Society. These are noted in the Byelaws of the Society.

Any member who is encountering difficulty in paying their subscription is encouraged to speak with the Treasurer in confidence.

Getting involved

There are many ways for members to get more involved in the activities of the Society. Ideas you may wish to consider include:

- Attending our scientific meetings
- Joining a specialist group of the Society
- Standing for election to the Board or one of the subcommittees
- Participating in Consensus or (short life working) groups
- Contributing to consultations and surveys
- Offering to host the annual meeting – this is a BIG but rewarding task. Ask the Honorary Secretary for more information, we have a 'guidebook' available for potential hosts and a professional company to assist with the logistics.

- Applying for a bursary or award.
- Helping to produce educational or other content for the society.
- Applying for a research grant.
- Presenting your research findings to the society.

Alliances with other societies

BSCOS has alliance agreement with the following societies:

- POSNA

- BOA

- EPOS

- APOS

- POSI

We also undertake joint working with other Specialist Societies.

The Board of Directors

BSCOS is strategically led by its elected Board of Directors who work within the company rules, set the Society byelaws and agree to abide by our Board and Members codes of conduct (see Appendix). It meets a minimum of three times per year and sets the framework for our Society's activities.

The Board has the following Directors:

- The President*
- The Honorary Secretary*
- The Treasurer*
- The President Elect (for the year immediately preceding Presidency)
- The Immediate Past President (for the year immediately following Presidency)
- 4 'Ordinary' members elected from the Society at large
- An 'Early years' member
- A lead for Equality, Diversity & Inclusion
- A member representing those working in a DGH setting.

*The President, Secretary and Treasurer are the 'Officers' of the Society.

Current Board members are listed with their contact details on the society website and are pleased to hear queries, suggestions and feedback from members.

The Board has close liaison with and receives reports from its subcommittees and specialist groups of the Society. In addition, the following may be invited to report at Board meetings:

- The Webadmin and Chair of the Publicity subcommittee
- The Chair of the Education subcommittee
- The Chair of the Research subcommittee

Those with an interest in serving the society on the Board are encouraged to discuss what is involved with a current Board member.

Only those members who are full (Ordinary) members in good standing may be elected to the Board.

Subcommittees of the Society

In recent years the Society has expanded its work in research and education, these efforts are led by respective subcommittees. We have also launched our publicity subcommittee to enable us to engage positively with social media.

Our subcommittees are the lifeblood of Society activity, meeting throughout the year to progress and serve the needs of members and wider society. Each subcommittee maintains open channels of communication with the Board to whom they are answerable, and report on their activities to members at our Annual meeting.

We rely on the membership to lead the Society forward through our committee structures. If you are interested in serving on one of these committees, please speak with the Chair of that committee or a current member to learn more about their work – see the list of contacts on the Society website.

Elections are held periodically to these subcommittees and are open to Ordinary and Associate and Affiliate members of the society who are in good standing.

Only Ordinary members may chair subcommittees of the society.

All subcommittees are expected to give consideration to issues of diversity and inclusion and to seek to integrate these principles where appropriate into their work.

Education subcommittee

The education subcommittee coordinates annual revalidation content in collaboration with the BOA at its meetings, supports local hosts in delivering the triannual current concepts course and supports local host with educational content at the BSCOS annual scientific meeting.

In recent times there has been an expansion into online educational content. This work is led by the educational subcommittee.

The Chair of the educational subcommittee (who must be an Ordinary Member) reports to meetings of the Board of Directors and at the Annual Scientific meeting of the Society.

See Society byelaws for terms of reference of the committee.

Research subcommittee

The Research subcommittee exists:

- to support and advise the BSCOS membership on research in paediatric orthopaedic surgery.
- to liaise with the BSCOS board on the direction and strategy of paediatric orthopaedic research in the UK.
- to develop research links with national and international organisations and funding bodies.

The committee helps to coordinate research efforts in paediatric orthopaedics and is responsible for the allocation of BSCOS pump-priming grants, when available.

The Chair of the research subcommittee (who must be an Ordinary member) reports to meetings of the Board of Directors and at the Annual Scientific meeting of the Society.

See Society byelaws for terms of reference of the committee.

Publicity subcommittee

The Publicity subcommittee leads on our web content and enables us to face challenges in communicating effectively both with each other and externally through social media as well as traditional media.

The Society Webadmin is a member of this committee (and may be its Chair) and reports to the Board.

The Chair of the Publicity subcommittee (who must be an Ordinary member) reports to meetings of the Board of Directors and at the Annual Scientific meeting of the Society.

See Society byelaws for terms of reference of the committee.

Reading committee

The reading committee assists the Board in scoring and ranking abstract submissions and bursary applications.

All Ordinary members of the society will be eligible to serve on the Reading subcommittee. There shall be up to 8 members of the Reading committee who are appointed for a 3-year term. Where there are more members who express a willingness to serve on this committee than there are vacancies, appointment shall be by random selection from amongst those who apply.

Members of the committee are appointed for a three-year term.

The reading committee does not send representation to the Board.

Specialist Groups

BSCOS recognises and supports several member-led specialist interest groups:

BSSCP

The British Society for Surgery in Cerebral Palsy is an informal group of Orthopaedic surgeons with a CP practice from across Europe who meet annually to consider member-generated research as well as case conferences. Speak to the Secretary of the society for more information.

UKCCG

The UK Clubfoot consensus group brings together a group of Orthopaedic surgeons with a keen interest in promoting Ponseti treatment for CTEV. Training courses are run in collaboration with Global Clubfoot.

SPOC

The Scottish Paediatric Orthopaedic Club brings together Children's Orthopaedic Surgeons north of the border for two meetings per year.

CPIPS/CPIPE

The Cerebral Palsy Integrated Pathway in Scotland was developed by SPOC in 2013 following the Swedish CPUP model, and offers a successful surveillance programme for children with CP. A similar programme has been rolled out in England and across the rest of the UK.

The Board is open to considering recognition of additional specialist groups if a group of members submit a plan.

Consensus & (Short Life) Working Groups

BSCOS supports the development of guidance and evidence based good practice.

We have previously reported on virtual fracture clinics, and recently through a specialist steering group we have collaborated with BASK in delivering recommendations on ACL and meniscal injury in the paediatric and adolescent population.

At the BSCOS AGM in Norwich, 2019, the membership voted in favour of a programme for BSCOS to establish guidelines for the management of common children's orthopaedic conditions. The guides should be consensus driven, not prescriptive and it is anticipated that they will contribute to reducing unjustifiable idiosyncratic variation in practice and might also support appraisal, the GIRFT process and promote education. The process is following a Delphi approach.

Consensus Steering Groups have been created for three areas of practice where consensus might be achieved most easily, namely:

• Management of DDH before 3 months old.

• Early management of osteo-articular infection in children.

• Management of clubfoot in the neonatal period.

It is hoped to build on these efforts with further areas of practice in due course.

These groups shall be subject to review on at least a quinquennial basis.

Membership of Consensus and Short life working groups of the Society is open to all Ordinary, Affiliate and Associate members in good standing.

Bursaries, Grants and Awards

As part of our ongoing commitment to education, BSCOS offers a number of awards to members. Details of application processes are found on the website, however an overview of the awards available follows here:

Medical Student Bursary

This Bursary is to support a medical undergraduate (usually a BSCOS member) in a UK Medical School with costs (up to £500) associated with either

- organising an elective placement relevant to the practice of children's orthopaedic surgery.
  or
- presenting a paper relevant to the practice of children's orthopaedic surgery at a national or international meeting.

Orthopaedic Trainee Bursary

This Bursary is to support the costs (up to £1000) incurred by a trainee (usually a BSCOS member) presenting a paper relevant to the practice of children's orthopaedic surgery at a scientific meeting.

Affiliate/Associate Member Bursary

This Bursary (of up to £1000) is available annually to assist an affiliate/associate* member of BSCOS in good standing to gain further knowledge that would benefit their paediatric orthopaedic (AHP) practice by visiting any centre in the UK or abroad. Attendance at formal training courses or meetings are excluded.

[* only Consultant and SASS doctors who are associate members may apply for this Bursary alongside affiliates]

Consultant Member Bursaries

Two Bursaries of up to £1000 are available annually to assist a Consultant (Ordinary) member of BSCOS in good standing to gain further knowledge that would benefit their paediatric orthopaedic practice by visiting a centre of excellence under the supervision of an expert in the field. Attendance at formal training courses or meetings are excluded.

Orthopediatrics Bursary

BSCOS, in association with Orthopediatrics offers a fellowship in children's orthopaedics in North America. The sponsorship is intended to support the professional development of surgeons primarily, but not exclusively, in their first five years of consultant practice. Its aims are to enhance their practice, establish and strengthen links and collaboration with the UK and North America. Orthopediatrics has agreed that if two candidates are equally deserving, the bursary may be divided evenly between them.

The successful applicant(s) would be able to visit

up to two departments in the US and/or Canada. Centres to be visited will be determined by their main clinical interest(s). Attendance of formal training courses or meetings at any centre will not be funded. The total sum of the Fellowship will not exceed US$10,000.00. If two candidates are selected they will be entitled to $5,000.00 each.

Applicants must be Ordinary members of BSCOS in good standing, have a substantial children's practice and be able to show evidence of publications in children's orthopaedics.

Research Grants

BSCOS may make available grants to Ordinary members of BSCOS in good standing for clinically focused pilot or feasibility studies that ideally will answer research questions in line with identified research priorities. These grants are designed to enable investigators to gather the data needed to move the research to the next stage. Ideally, this is intended to be pump-prime funding and applicants are asked to outline how they will leverage the grant to obtain further funding from external funding bodies.

Further details are available on application to the Research Committee Chair although a call will be made when grants become available.

Additionally, support may be made available for statistical advice for research undertaken by Ordinary members in good standing.

In all cases grants and awards may only be applied for by member(s) in good standing.

BJJ Prize

This Prize for the best paper presented at the Annual Scientific Meeting will be awarded by the Society.

By accepting the prize, the authors of the winning paper agree that the paper will be submitted to BJJ for peer review within 3 months and will not be subsequently withdrawn for any reason.

The prize will be awarded to the lead author. It is understood by all authors that the prize is for the paper, not for any one contribution to it.

The authors and their institution should decide what to do with the prize.

The authors agree to submit a photograph from the meeting along with a summary/abstract of the winning paper to BJJ News, regardless of whether their paper is accepted for the BJJ.

Appendix I: Company Rules

British Society for Children's Orthopaedic Surgery
(Company Limited by Guarantee number SC465033)
Company Rules

Registered address: British Society for Children's Orthopaedic Surgery, 25 Castle Terrace, Edinburgh, EH1 2ER. Company Limited by Guarantee.

bscos.org.uk

These Rules were adopted in accordance with Article 20 of the Company's Articles of Incorporation on 1st September 2016 as amended 25th April 2021.

Membership of the Society

a. Ordinary Membership shall be open to Consultant Orthopaedic Surgeons working in the United Kingdom, who have a special interest in orthopaedic problems relating to children and who commit a significant proportion of their clinical time to dealing with such matters. Where possible, they should have demonstrated their interest in children's orthopaedics and fracture management by research and publication. Application for Ordinary Membership shall be made to the Secretary. It must be accompanied by a curriculum vitae and supported by two referees who are already Members of the Society and in good standing. Where an application has been approved by the Board of Directors, it will be announced to the Society Members.

Ordinary Membership will cease on receipt of a member's written resignation, or if there is a failure to pay the annual subscription.

It is expected that a Member will attend the Society's annual scientific meeting or an Allied Society meeting regularly. Membership will cease if a Member has not attended a relevant scientific meeting for three consecutive years.

b. Overseas Membership shall be available to Ordinary Members who are working abroad, have a special interest in orthopaedic problems relating to children and who continue to commit a significant proportion of their clinical time to dealing with such matters. Application for Overseas Membership shall be made to the Secretary. It must be accompanied by a curriculum vitae and supported by two referees who are already Members of the Society and in good standing. Where an application has been approved by the Board of Directors it will be announced to the Society Members.

Overseas Membership will cease on receipt of a Member's written resignation or where there is a failure to pay the annual subscription.

c. Honorary Membership may be offered to distinguished surgeons and scientists who have a special interest in children's orthopaedics. Recommendations may be made either by the Board of Directors, or to the Board of Directors by 20 Members, and will be approved at the Annual General Meeting of the Society.

d. The Board may determine other categories of membership (non-voting) at its discretion. Details of these membership categories can be found in the Company Byelaws.

e. The Board of Directors shall retain the right to exercise discretion over extraordinary matters in respect of Society Membership.

The Board of Directors

The Board of Directors shall comprise the President, Honorary Secretary, Honorary Treasurer, the President Elect, the Immediate Past President, one 'Early Years member', one Diversity & Inclusion lead, one DGH member and four 'Ordinary members'.

Ordinary (or exceptionally other Board members) may be co-opted onto sub-committees and/or sub-committee leads may be invited to the Board to facilitate liaison between the Board and its sub-committees.

The President, Honorary Secretary and Honorary Treasurer are the Officers of the Society.

Upon completion of the term of office or resignation of the relevant incumbent director:

a. The **President elect** shall be elected one year in advance of taking up the post of President. They shall be elected by the Ordinary members at large, from amongst those voting members of the Board willing to serve, who have completed at least one year on the Board (and/or are within three years of leaving the Board).

b. The **President** shall serve for a period of two years upon completion of their term as President elect. The President where possible shall chair all meetings of the Board. In his/her absence the Immediate Past president or President Elect or in their absence one of the other officers shall assume the chair.

c. The **Immediate past president** shall serve one further year as a Board member upon completion of their term as President of the Board.

d. The **Honorary Secretary** and **Honorary Treasurer** shall be elected by the ordinary members at large from amongst those voting members of the Board of Directors who are willing to serve and shall hold office for a period of two years, they shall be eligible for re-election for one further year only.

e. There shall be four **Ordinary members** proposed from amongst and elected by the Ordinary members at large of the Society. They shall hold office for three years, fulfilling a liaison role with the subcommittees of the Board. They may stand for re-election to this role for one further term.

f. There shall be an **Early Years member** of the Board who shall be within 10 years of appointment proposed from amongst Ordinary members of the Society to the Consultant grade on the date nominations are requested and shall be elected by the Ordinary members at large of the Society. They shall hold office for

3 years and may not stand for re-election to this role (but may stand subsequently for election as an Ordinary member).

g. There shall be a **Diversity & Inclusion member** of the Board proposed from amongst and elected by the Ordinary members at large of the Society. They shall hold office for three years, and may stand for re-election to this role for one further term.

h. There shall be a **DGH member** of the Board proposed from amongst those who work predominantly outside of tertiary children's centres, and elected by the Ordinary members at large of the Society. They shall hold office for three years, and may stand for re-election to this role for one further term.

The Board of Directors shall have the power to co-opt additional non-voting Members where appropriate.

The following may be invited to attend the Board on a non-voting basis for the period of their tenure in that role:

i. The Webadmin &/or The Chair of the Publicity subcommittee
ii. The Chair of the Education subcommittee
iii. The Chair of the Research subcommittee

All members are expected to adhere to the Society's Code of Conduct.

Voting in Committee

In the event of a vote being required for Board of Directors matters, each Director shall have a vote. Invitees, Co-opted Members. In the event of a tie, the President's decision will be binding.

Meetings of the Board

The Board of Directors shall meet three times a year; at the Annual Society Spring Meeting, in the Summer and in the Autumn. Matters of urgent and/or confidential business may be considered at the discretion of the President with advice of other Officers of the Society between meetings of the Board. The President may convene extraordinary meetings as deemed necessary. Online meetings shall be considered equally valid as those in-person for Board decisions.

All meetings of the Board shall be intimated to its members with no less than 6 weeks notice, unless all voting Board members mutually agree to a shorter notice period.

Elections to the Board

Elections shall normally take place when an incumbent Board Director's tenure is completed. Where a Board Director's position otherwise falls vacant, there shall be an election to that vacancy on the same basis as if the tenure had been completed.

The Honorary Secretary shall act as Returning officer for elections to the Board, or in their absence the Immediate past president shall take on this responsibility.

Eligible members of the Society shall be notified of Board elections within a maximum of 3 months of a position falling vacant. There shall be a minimum period of 1 month allowed for nominations to be received.

Only members in good standing may self-nominate for a position.

Elections shall be open and transparent, according to the timetable and process set out by the Returning officer in advance of each election. The results shall be published and made available to Ordinary members of the Society.

Quorum

The Board shall be quorate with a minimum of one officer and five other voting members present.

Subcommittees of the Board

The Board may establish at its discretion subcommittees and working groups, devolving authority to these groups within a remit established by the Board which will nevertheless retain responsibility for and oversight of all the Society's activities.

The Chairs of the Research, Education, Publicity (and any other) subcommittees may be invited to attend Board meetings at the Board's discretion.

An Ordinary member of the Board may be appointed to act as liaison and sit as an observer at subcommittee meetings.

Meetings of the Society

i. *Scientific Meetings*. The Society will meet at a date and venue recommended by the Board of Directors and approved at the Annual General Meeting. Scientific Meetings of the Society shall be open to all Members. A charge, set by the Board, may be levied for attendance. Non-Members may attend at the invitation of a Member and will be charged an entry fee. An attendance register shall be prepared by the local host and shall be passed to the Honorary Secretary.

ii. *The Annual General Meeting* shall be held during the Scientific Meeting of the Society.

The President or, in his/her absence the Secretary, shall take the Chair. The Treasurer shall present a report on the Society's financial standing. Postal and/or online ballots will be arranged for those matters requiring a decision by the Membership.

Ordinary, Overseas and Honorary Members may attend and have voting privileges.

Associate members who are Consultants, Staff Grade, Associate Specialist & Specialty doctors may attend the AGM but shall not have voting privileges.

Affiliate members are not permitted to attend the AGM of the society nor do they have voting privileges.

iii An *Extraordinary General Meeting* may be called by the Board at its discretion with a minimum of 6 weeks notice to the Ordinary members at large.

A group consisting of at least fifteen percent of Ordinary members in good standing may require such a meeting to be organised for a specific item of business.

Subscriptions

There will be an annual subscription. Ordinary and Overseas Members shall pay a full subscription. Honorary Members are exempt. Upon application, the Board shall have discretion to waive the fees for Overseas members who are working in a fully charitable capacity in low and middle income countries.

Subscriptions for other (non-voting) categories of membership shall be determined by the Board and approved at the annual meeting of the Society.

In the event of a member failing to pay the appropriate subscription in full within 3 months of the due date, that membership shall expire with immediate effect. Thereafter, a new formal application for membership following the relevant process would need to be submitted for readmission to the society.

Amendment(s) to the Company Rules

Notice of any proposed change(s) by members at large must be made at least 28 days before the next Annual General Meeting to the Honorary Secretary and should be supported by at least fifteen percent of Ordinary Members in good standing.

The Board may, at their discretion, recommend changes to the Company Rules with a minimum of 28 days notice to members of a vote on the proposed changes by postal or electronic ballot. Such a vote must be stayed if a valid requirement for an extraordinary general meeting (see above) is made about such recommendations.

ANNEX

1. ACCEA

The Society will act as a specialist society according to ACCEA, and will support its Members according to the rules and guidelines laid down by that organisation.

Appendix II: Society Byelaws

- Byelaws of the Society may not contravene the Company Rules and should be read in conjunction with them.
- In all matters of dispute, the Board interpretation of the Society Byelaws shall be final.

i Membership of the Society

In addition to Ordinary, Overseas and Honorary Members who have voting rights according to the Constitution, BSCOS recognises the following additional (non-voting) categories of membership:

a. Associate Membership

This category of membership is open to:

- *Consultant Surgeons from other disciplines and those with locum Orthopaedic Consultant posts who commit a proportion of their clinical time to the management of musculoskeletal conditions in children.

- *Staff grade, Associate Specialist & Specialty (SASS) Doctors who commit a proportion of their clinical time to the management of children with conditions that result in regular work alongside children's orthopaedic surgeons
- Trainees in orthopaedic surgery in possession of a national training number
- Doctors on the specialist register for trauma and orthopaedics practising as Fellows in children's orthopaedic surgery

Associate members (excluding those who do not hold a substantive career grade post) may stand for election to subcommittees and working groups of the Society but may not chair subcommittees.

*Consultant and SASS doctor associate members may attend but not vote at the AGM of the Society.

Applicants should be proposed and seconded by Members of the Society as described above. Where an application has been approved by the Board of Directors, it will be announced to the Society Members at the next Annual Meeting. For those in a training or locum post, the tenure of their Associate Membership will be the duration of the training or locum post and for a maximum of five years. For those holding substantive appointments, Associate Membership is not time-limited.

Where an Associate Member has been appointed to a substantive Consultant Orthopaedic appointment with a special interest in orthopaedic problems relating to children and where they will commit a significant proportion of their clinical time to dealing with such matters, they shall no longer be eligible for Associate Membership and shall need to apply to transfer to become an Ordinary Member.

Associate Membership will cease on receipt of a Member's written resignation, or if there is a failure to pay the annual subscription or transfer when no longer eligible to hold this category of membership.

Associate Membership will also cease if the Member has not attended a relevant scientific meeting for three consecutive years.

b. Affiliate Membership

Affiliate membership is available for appropriately qualified allied health professionals who regularly treat children in an orthopaedic capacity, surgical or otherwise. It is expected that this aspect of their work is carried out in conjunction with Ordinary Members of the Society. A letter of application should be sent to the Honorary Secretary together with a current Curriculum Vitae and supporting references from 2 Ordinary Members of the Society in good standing. Where an application has been approved by the Board of Directors, it will be announced to the Society Members at the next Annual Meeting.

Affiliate Membership will cease on receipt of a

member's written resignation, or if there is a failure to pay the annual subscription.

Affiliate Membership will also cease if the Member has not attended a scientific meeting for three consecutive years.

Affiliate members may stand for election to Consensus/working groups and subcommittees of the Society but are not eligible to chair these groups.

c. Medical Student Membership

Medical student membership is available at the discretion of the Board for motivated medical students studying in a UK Medical School. It is expected that they would have formed a strong interest in children's orthopaedic surgery during their undergraduate training. A letter of application should be sent to the Honorary Secretary together with a current Curriculum Vitae and supporting references from 2 Ordinary Members of the Society in good standing. Where an application has been approved by the Board of Directors, it will be announced to the Society Members at the next Annual Meeting. Medical Student Membership will cease on receipt of a member's written resignation, or where there is a failure to pay the annual subscription for two consecutive years. Medical Student Membership will also cease when the student completes their undergraduate degree when they will have the opportunity to apply for Associate Membership of the Society.

d. Honorary International Membership

The Board has discretion to grant Honorary International Membership to any individual who has made an outstanding contribution to the field of Orthopaedic Surgery and specifically aligned with the aims of BSCOS.

Honorary International Membership does not attract a membership fee and does not carry the voting privileges of Ordinary membership.

Subscriptions

The Board shall set subscription rates which shall be reviewed upon the recommendation of the Treasurer and published at the AGM for the approval of the Society.

The following are the fees accepted at the AGM of 2021 and remain extant until further review takes place.

The full subscription payable per annum (in 2022) is £100 on the following basis:

Ordinary Member	Full fee (100%)
Honorary Member	Nil
Associate Member	Reduced fee (50%)
Affiliate Member	Reduced fee (25%)
Medical Student Member	Reduced fee (10%)
Overseas Member	Full fee (100%)
Honorary International Member	Nil

Transfer of membership category

Where a member of any category of membership changes their status (for example, where a Trainee who is an Associate member takes up a Consultant post), the member shall be required to notify the secretary of the date of that change within a 3 month period, and comply with any requirements of their new status within a total of 6 months from the date of change. In particular, the correct subscription must be paid in full on the next anniversary of membership following the change. Failure to do so shall result in expiry of membership with immediate effect. Thereafter, a new formal application for membership would need to be submitted for readmission to the Society.

ii Subcommittees of the Society

a) Education Subcommittee

The Education subcommittee shall be appointed from career grade Ordinary, Affiliate & Associate Members of the society subject to application.

The Education Lead shall be appointed to Chair the Education Subcommittee from amongst its ordinary members, subject to ratification by the Board. They shall have responsibility for the organisation of the instructional programme of BOA meetings and represent the Society in the educational domain.

The Education subcommittee is expected to act within its terms of reference and is accountable to the Board.

TERMS OF REFERENCE

Objectives

- To support and advise BSCOS membership on education in paediatric orthopaedic surgery.
- To liaise with the BSCOS board on the direction and strategy of paediatric orthopaedic education in the UK.
- To coordinate the educational activities of the Society.

Responsibilities

- Supporting the educational content of the BSCOS annual meeting.
- Organisation of the paediatric orthopaedic revalidation section of the BOA Annual Congress.
- Organisation and support of the 3 yearly Current Concepts Course.
- Coordinating Surgeon and Patient information.

- Collation of currently available policy documents and information sheets.
- To liaise with the Publicity Committee and maintain open channels of communication with them.

Membership

- The Education committee (EC) will consist of up to 8 members.
- Quorum for each meeting to be a minimum of 4 members, one of whom must be the chair.
- All members should be full and active members of BSCOS.
- The term of office for members will be three years. Members can seek reappointment for a further term (maximum 2 terms).
- Applications for membership will be sought by the BSCOS Board from eligible members of BSCOS as and when new members are required on the EC.

- The committee shall have the capacity to co-opt up to one additional member where that would bring additional skills and competencies.

Chair

- The chair will be proposed by the EC, must be an ordinary member of the society and is subject to approval by the BSCOS Board.
- The term of office is three years and the chair can seek reappointment for a further term (maximum of 2 terms).

Accountability

- The Board shall maintain close interest in the Committee's work.
- Accountability is to the BSCOS board through reporting by the Chair.
- The Board can appoint one of its members to liaise with the committee

and has observer status on the committee.

- Activities of the Committee are subject to review by the Board, although in general it will act with autonomy within its remit.

Frequency of Meetings

- The Education Committee will conduct business by quarterly teleconferences and meet formally at the BSCOS annual conference.

b) Research Subcommittee

The Research subcommittee shall be appointed from the Ordinary, Affiliate & Associate Members of the society subject to application.

The Research Lead shall be appointed to Chair the Research Subcommittee from amongst its ordinary members, subject to ratification by the

Board. The Research Lead shall be responsible for the representation of all matters relating to research that involve the Society including international, national and multicentre collaborative studies.

The Research subcommittee is expected to act within its terms of reference and is accountable to the Board.

TERMS OF REFERENCE

Objectives

- To support and advise the BSCOS membership on research in paediatric orthopaedic surgery.
- To liaise with the BSCOS board on the direction and strategy of paediatric orthopaedic research in the UK.
- To develop research links with national and international organisations and funding bodies.

Responsibilities

- Provide professional advice and guidance for BSCOS members who have an interest carrying out prospective research in paediatric orthopaedic surgery.
- Review projects submitted via a standardised 'PICO' form published on the BSCOS website.
- Develop the priorities for paediatric orthopaedic research and communicate this with the membership and funding bodies.
- Explore avenues of funding.
- Spread awareness of current and future research projects and disseminate results to BSCOS members and beyond.
- Suggest expert reviewers to funding bodies for grant applications in subject relevant areas.

Membership

- The research committee (RC) will consist of up to 8 members.
- Quorum for each meeting to be a minimum of 4 members, one of whom must be the chair.
- The RC has the freedom to co-opt a lay patient/carer representative. The RC can liaise with the various charities to seek suitable volunteers.
- All members except for the patient/carer representative should be full and active members of BSCOS.
- The term of office for members will be three years. Members can seek reappointment for a further term (maximum 2 terms).
- Applications for membership will be sought by the BSCOS Board from eligible members of BSCOS as and when new members are required on the RC. It would be expected that there would be representation from both university and NHS employed consultants.

- The committee shall have the capacity to co-opt up to one additional member where that would bring additional skills and competencies.

Chair

- The chair will be an ordinary member of the society proposed by the RC and is subject to the approval of the BSCOS Board.
- The term of office is three years and the chair can seek re-election for a further term (maximum of 2 terms).

Accountability

- The Board shall maintain close interest in the Committee's work.
- Accountability is to the BSCOS board through reporting by the Chair.
- The Board can appoint one of its members to liaise with the committee

and has observer status on the committee.

- Activities of the Committee are subject to review by the Board, although in general it will act with autonomy within its remit.

Frequency of Meetings

- The RC will meet every 6 months with further meetings arranged if required.

c) Publicity Subcommittee

The Publicity subcommittee shall be appointed from Ordinary, Affiliate & Associate Members of the society subject to application.

The Publicity Lead shall be appointed to Chair the Publicity Subcommittee from amongst its ordinary members, subject to ratification by the Board. The Publicity Lead shall be responsible for Society communications with BSCOS members and externally where appropriate.

The webadmin shall be a member of the Publicity subcommittee and may (if also an ordinary member) be its chair.

The Publicity subcommittee is expected to act within its terms of reference and is accountable to the Board.

TERMS OF REFERENCE

Objectives

- To use the BSCOS website and other social media channels to inform the members of BSCOS, other medical professionals and the general public of the activities of the society and to deliver educational material.
- To liaise with the BSCOS board regarding the methods of promotion to be used.
- To foster links within the society and between BSCOS and others involved in

216

the care of orthopaedic diagnoses in children

Responsibilities

- To explore and enhance methods for sharing information with the Society and others to whom it may be of interest
- To develop and strengthen the presence of BSCOS on social media
- To agree and publicise standards to be applied before sharing any information on the website or social media channels
- To share proposed content with the Board at a minimum of 1 week before it is to be released.
- To liaise with the Publicity Committee and maintain open channels of communication with them.

Membership

- The Publicity committee (PC) will consist of up to 8 members.
- Quorum for each meeting to be a minimum of 3 members, one of whom must be the chair.
- All members should be full and active members of BSCOS.
- The term of office for members will be three years. Members can seek reappointment for a further term (maximum 2 terms).
- Applications for membership will be sought by the BSCOS Board from eligible members of BSCOS as and when new members are required on the PC.

- The committee shall have the capacity to co-opt up to one additional member where that would bring additional skills and competencies.

Chair

- The chair will be proposed by the PC Com and will usually be the BSCOS Webadmin. The post will be approved by the BSCOS Board.
- The Board shall maintain close interest in the Committee's work by means of a representative from one sitting on the other as determined by the Board.
- The term of office is three years, and the chair can seek reappointment for a further term (maximum of 2 terms).
- The Chair shall be the responsible person in respect of GDPR compliance for the society.

Accountability

- The Board shall maintain close interest in the Committee's work.
- Accountability is to the BSCOS board through reporting by the Chair.

- The Board will appoint one of its members to liaise with the committee and has observer status on the committee.
- Activities of the Publicity Committee are subject to review by the Board, although in general it will act with autonomy within its remit.

Frequency of Meetings

- The PC Com will meet quarterly with further meetings arranged if required.

d) Reading committee

We are grateful to members of this subcommittee who assist the Board in scoring and ranking abstract submissions and bursary applications.

All Ordinary members of the society will be eligible to serve on the Reading committee.

There shall be up to 8 members of the Reading committee who are appointed for a 3 year term.

Where there are more members who express a willingness to serve on this committee than there are vacancies, appointment shall be by random selection from amongst those who apply.

The reading committee does not elect a chair and does not send representation to the Board.

iii Specified Roles within the Society

President

The President of the Society shall represent the Society and shall Chair its Board of Directors, leading the strategic direction of the Society.

With the Treasurer and Secretary, as Officers of the Society, they shall take particular responsibility for fulfilling the legal obligations of the Society.

221

Immediate Past President/President Elect

The Immediate Past President/President Elect shall act in an advisory capacity to support their successor in post. They shall chair meetings of the Board which the President is unable to attend.

Shall usually act as a link with other societies including the BOA.

Honorary Secretary

The Honorary Secretary shall be responsible for:
- organisation of Board meetings
- agenda setting (with the President) and distribution of papers to Directors.
- keeping the authorised minute of Board and General Meeting business.
- receiving and processing applications to join the Society.

- the timely consideration of applications for Bursaries and Grants awarded by the Society.
- receiving communications to the Board.
- issuing decisions made by the Board.
- acting as Returning Officer for elections of the Society.

With the President and Treasurer, as Officers of the Society, they shall take particular responsibility for fulfilling the legal obligations of the Society.

Honorary Treasurer

The Honorary Treasurer shall be responsible for:
- Maintaining the bank account(s) of the Society.
- Recommending subscription rates to the Board of Directors
- Corresponding with members concerning agreed subscription rates.

- Reporting on financial performance of the Society to its Board and General Meetings.
- Authorising and processing claims for expenses
- Acting with fiscal prudence and maintaining appropriate counter-fraud and other security measures over the financial resources of the Society.
- Liaison with our Accountants to ensure timely production of the Accounts for Board approval and submission to Companies House.
- Ensuring that appropriate insurance(s) are in place for the Society in respect of its activities and those acting on its behalf in an official capacity.

With the President and Secretary, as Officers of the Society, they shall take particular responsibility for fulfilling the legal obligations of the Society.

Webadmin

The webadmin in their ex-officio capacity shall be responsible for:
- Maintaining the website of the Society as directed by the Board
- Sharing Board communications with the membership
- Running online processes for payment of subscriptions (on behalf of and in liaison with the Treasurer).
- Running online processes for elections (on the instruction of and in liaison with the Returning officer (Hon Secretary) of the Society).
- Recommending appropriate investment in technology and software to the Board in support of the activities of the society.
- Maintain registration with the ICO.
- Maintaining and monitoring compliance of the society with its own GDPR policy and the legal requirements that underpin it.

Diversity & Inclusion Lead

The following remit shall be held by the DI lead, although all Society members are expected to play their part in upholding and promoting the values of the Society.

- The DI Lead shall seek to promote the principles of equality, diversity and inclusion in the activities of the society.
- To instil appropriate regard to equality of treatment of all members and participants in respect of protected as well as other characteristics which might otherwise be a source of inappropriate discrimination in all activities of the society.
- To actively explore the development of a range of activities such as buddying and mentoring schemes which encourage women and under-represented groups of clinicians to apply for leadership roles within the Society.

- To monitor the messaging of Society projects, both internally and externally, to ensure that they are inclusive.
- To monitor the demographics of the society and make report to the Board (and the society as a whole) of the impact of efforts to address issues relating to Equality, Diversity and Inclusion.
- To have responsibility for educational content of the society in respect of diversity and inclusion.

DGH Board member

This Board member shall be elected from amongst those Ordinary members who work predominantly outside of tertiary children's centres. The DGH board member shall have a lead role to

- act as a link for the Board for all issues relevant to those working in these centres.
- maintain awareness of the needs of those working in these centres to

ensure equitable access to paediatric orthopaedic care across the UK.
- bring relevant medico-political issues and devolved national issues to the attention of the Board and Society.

iv Miscellaneous policies & rules for all Board Subcommittees and working groups

- For any queries regarding the remit of a given committee please contact either the President (president@bscos.org.uk) or the Secretary (secretary@bscos.org.uk).
- Any and all external communications from a group/committee that lie outside the remit of the group/committee must be first discussed with the President/Secretary.
- Committee communications - The BSCOS webadmin (webadmin@bscos.org.uk) will be able to provide an email for use by approved groups, as well as offering advice on

videoconferencing and survey capacity etc) that may be available to facilitate your group/committee.

- Reports/updates of committee work should be submitted to the Board via the Secretary in time for Board meetings at which the Chair of the group may also be required to make a verbal report.
- Each committee or group chair shall make effort to ensure that EDI principles are upheld and GDPR requirements are fulfilled in all of its activities. Queries for EDI should be directed to the EDI Lead. Queries for GDPR should be directed to the webadmin in the first instance.
- Logistics:
  - Whilst it is anticipated there is likely to be value in and need for initial (and subsequent) face to face meetings of groups/committees, use of VC working is encouraged both for reasons of inclusion of participants for whom travel is

less easy and to minimise cost to
the society.
- ○ Wherever possible there should
  be provision for remote
  participation in all face to face
  meetings.
- ○ Any group who the Board
  approves to meet on behalf of
  BSCOS may approach the
  Treasurer in advance for a
  budget to support their
  activities, within the agreed
  Society expenses rules.
- ○ It is usual for the chair of a
  group/committee to plan, book
  and pay for any such meeting
  and seek reimbursement
  thereafter. Reimbursement for
  non-personal meetings expenses
  should be submitted via the link
  on the BSCOS website available
  on request from the Treasurer.
- Expenses:
  - ○ All BSCOS activities are required
    to adhere to agreed fiscal
    controls.

o   Any expense queries should be
    raised with the Treasurer
    (treasurer@bscos.org.uk).

o   Please draw the committee
    members' attention to the rules
    surrounding expenses before
    any such expenses are incurred.
    Retrospective permission for
    expenses outwith the rules is
    very unlikely to be granted.

o   The chair of a group shall be
    responsible for confirming the
    attendance of members of the
    group at a given meeting to the
    Treasurer within a week of the
    meeting to allow the Treasurer
    to reimburse verified claims on a
    timely basis.

o   The Board Treasurer will
    monitor expenses for a given
    group or committee and feed
    any issues back to the Chair of
    that group and to the Board.

v Personal Expenses

Expenses incurred as a result of work on behalf of the Society will generally be reimbursed if the following rules are observed:

- The online form provided shall be used to claim expenses for approved meetings of the Board or its subcommittees, or when attending other meetings when recognized as a delegate of the Board.
- Claim forms must be accompanied by (copy) receipts in order to be honoured (excepting personal mileage or oyster fares).
- Claims are only paid in respect of personal expenses incurred. Expenses for family members or dependents or colleagues cannot be paid.
- Payment will be by electronic transfer to the bank details provided.
- All claims should be submitted within 3 months of the meeting or event for which they were incurred (although

significant expense items may be submitted in advance).

- Claimants attention is drawn to the following specific guidance in respect of expense types.
- Expenses incurred in respect of Board subcommittees or other recognised groups must be identified as such. The Chair of each subcommittee is required to ensure that the subcommittee adheres to the identified budget for a given area of work.
- Where a member is unsure if there is a budget for an expense they are strongly advised to check with the chair of the group and/or the Treasurer to gain authorisation in advance of committing to the expenditure.
- **Any exceptional expenses or deviation from this guidance must be pre-authorised by the Treasurer or the expense cannot be paid.**

Air travel

- Flights under 5 hours will be reimbursed to the maximum level of the applicable BA economy fare.
- Flights 5 hours and over will be reimbursed to the maximum level of the BA premium economy fare.
- The use of advance discount tickets is encouraged, the expense can be claimed as soon as it is incurred.

Personal mileage
- This will be reimbursed at a rate set in line with the BMA rate (45p per mile).

Rail travel
- Journeys of one hour or less are reimbursed at standard class rates only
- Journeys of over one hour may be first class
- The use of advance discount tickets is encouraged, the expense can be claimed as soon as it is incurred.

Accommodation

- Overnight stay will only be reimbursed where the journey from home would need to start before 6am or return home would be after 11pm in order to attend the meeting.
- The use of advanced discounts and competitive hotel rates is encouraged.
- Where overnight stay is necessary, this will be reimbursed to a maximum of set in line with the BMA rate (£195 per night).

Subsistence

- Where overnight stay is necessary or arrival to home is later than 9pm, dinner expenses may be claimed to a maximum of £35.

(Personal) conference expenses

- The society does **not** reimburse its own members (of any membership category) for any expenses incurred when attending its educational events

(Scientific meetings, Current Concepts, BOA or other events).

- Invited guest speakers (who are not BSCOS members) shall be reimbursed at the personal expense rates determined by the society in its byelaws.

(Organiser) conference expenses

- Budgeted expenses for BSCOS conferences and events will be reimbursed to organisers upon production of relevant receipts using the online form:

MEETING **VENUE EXPENSES LINK**

- Expenses may also be directly paid by invoice in liaison with the Treasurer.
- Organisers are required to remain within budget and liaise closely with the Treasurer.

vi Bursary & Fellowship rules & claims

Bursaries, fellowships and awards are made by decision of the Board of Directors.
Application for a Bursary, award or fellowship shall constitute agreement to be bound by the rules governing them.

The Board of Directors decision is final in respect of awards made.

Those awarded bursaries shall be subject to the rules governing them:

a) Orthopediatrics Fellowship x1 or 2

Eligibility:
- Consultant Orthopaedic Surgeon
- Ordinary Member in good standing with BSCOS at time of application

Application:
- The timing and requirements of application are as posted on the BSCOS website and subject to the final decision of the Board.

Conditions:

- Funds should not be committed until the Hon Secretary has confirmed the award in writing (or by email).
- Unless agreed otherwise, the fellowship is to be completed before the next annual Spring meeting of the Society.
- The recipient commits to attend and present at the next annual Society meeting following the award.
- The funds are solely for the personal travel, accommodation and subsistence of the recipient.
- The total award will not exceed the GBP equivalent of US$ 10,000 at the time the award is claimed
- The recipient shall present PDF copies (or posted original) receipts for all items claimed together.
- A letter of thanks from the recipient to Orthopediatrics for the award would be considered appropriate.
- Personal mileage will be paid at the BMA rate (45p per mile in 2016-17).

- When converting from foreign currency, please use the exchange rate at the time the expense was incurred.
- Expenses should be claimed together within 3 months of return from the fellowship.
- At the discretion of the Board the award may be shared between 2 recipients of merit. In this situation, neither applicant can expect their reimbursement to exceed the equivalent of US$ 5,000.

b) Consultant Bursary x2

Eligibility:
- Consultant Orthopaedic Surgeon
- Full Member in good standing with BSCOS at time of application

Application:
- The timing and requirements of application are as posted on the BSCOS

website and subject to the final decision of the Board.

Conditions:
- Funds should not be committed until the Hon Secretary has confirmed the award in writing (or by email).
- Unless agreed otherwise, the bursary is to be completed before the next annual Spring meeting of the Society.
- The funds are solely for the personal travel, accommodation and subsistence of the recipient.
- The total award will not exceed £1000
- The recipient shall present PDF copies (or posted original) receipts for all items claimed together.
- The award will be paid into a nominated bank account
- The recipient must present at the next Society meeting

c) Trainee Bursary x1

Eligibility:

- Specialist Registrar (or equivalent) in Orthopaedic Surgery (usually a BSCOS member) in order to present a paper on the theme of Children's Orthopaedics at a scientific meeting where alternative funding is not forthcoming.

Application:

- The timing and requirements of application are as posted on the BSCOS website and subject to the final decision of the Board.

Conditions:

- Funds should not be committed until the Hon Secretary has confirmed the award in writing (or by email).
- The funds are solely for personal costs (conference fee, travel, accommodation and subsistence of the recipient) for which alternative funding has not been forthcoming.

- The total award will not exceed £1000
- The recipient shall present PDF copies (or posted original) receipts for all items claimed together.
- The award will be paid into a nominated bank account.

d) Affiliate/Associate member Bursary x1

Eligibility:
- Affiliate member of BSCOS in good standing at the time of application
- Associate member (Consultant/SSAS doctor) of BSCOS in good standing at the time of application

Application:
- The timing and requirements of application are as posted on the BSCOS website and subject to the final decision of the Board.

Conditions:

- Funds should not be committed until the Hon Secretary has confirmed the award in writing (or by email).
- The funds are solely for personal costs (travel, accommodation and subsistence of the recipient) for which alternative funding has not been forthcoming.
- The total award will not exceed £1000
- The recipient shall present PDF copies (or posted original) receipts for all items claimed together.
- The award will be paid into a nominated bank account.

e) Medical Student Bursary x1

Eligibility:

- Medical Student (usually a BSCOS member) to assist with expenses incurred in attending to present a paper on a topic related to paediatric orthopaedic surgery or an elective

associated with paediatric orthopaedic
surgery.

Application:
- The timing and requirements of
  application are as posted on the BSCOS
  website and subject to the final decision
  of the Board.

Conditions:
- Funds should not be committed until
  the Hon Secretary has confirmed the
  award in writing (or by email).
- The funds are solely for personal costs
  (conference fee, travel, accommodation
  and subsistence of the recipient) for
  which alternative funding has not been
  forthcoming.
- The total award will not exceed £500
- The recipient shall present PDF copies
  (or posted original) receipts for all items
  claimed together.
- The award will be paid into a nominated
  bank account.

vi Conference & Event refund/cancellation policy

Subject to any published specific provisions for a given event, the following policy shall apply:

1.   Refunds for tickets purchased in respect of BSCOS events will not generally be available from a point less than 6 weeks before the date of the event and may be less than what was paid where costs cannot be recouped or the ticket cannot be resold.

2.   Where an event has been cancelled, BSCOS will endeavour to offer an alternative date for the event for which the ticket will be valid.

3.   Ticket refunds (for Conference and where applicable for a dinner) at face value will be available on request when an event has been cancelled by BSCOS. The request must be submitted within 3 months of the cancelled event and will generally be refunded to the same account from which the payment was made.

4. Regrettably, BSCOS cannot be responsible for any other consequential expenses incurred. Where possible it is suggested that a refund is sought from credit card companies or other travel insurance held.

5. Refunded delegates should be aware that there may subsequently be a rise in fees for a (rescheduled) conference from which they will not be protected.

Conference sponsorship cancellation and refund policy

1. Refunds for sponsorship in respect of BSCOS events will not generally be available.

2. Where an event has been cancelled, BSCOS will endeavour to offer an alternative date for the event to which the sponsor is invited to carry forward their sponsorship.

3. Sponsor refunds will be available on request when an event has been cancelled by BSCOS. The request must be submitted within 3

months of the cancelled event and will require a letter to the Treasurer detailing the account into which any refund should be made.

4.   A refunded sponsor shall have no guarantee of access to a subsequent (rescheduled) event.

vii Code of conduct

The Society seeks to operate in an atmosphere of trust, kindness and mutual respect.

Members of BSCOS, attendees at its meetings and anyone acting on behalf of the Society agree to be bound by the following code of conduct:

Conflicts of interest

Members and participants in the activities of the society do so on the basis of mutual trust. A conflict of interest arises when a member (or participant) has an interest in a subject which may, or could reasonably be perceived to, inappropriately limit or introduce bias to the objectivity, rigour or scope of their participation.

There is a responsibility upon all members to where possible avoid, and otherwise to declare (potential) conflicts of interest in advance of any topic being discussed.

In consultation with attendees, the Chair of committee or Lead for a given meeting/activity shall determine whether the conflict should affect participation in the discussion. The decision may be to:

a) dismiss the (potential) conflict as not likely to be a significant factor

b) note the (potential) conflict but permit ongoing participation nevertheless

c) recuse the individual(s) involved for the discussion &/or decision on relevant topic(s).

Any possible conflicts should be recorded clearly on a slide in presentations.

Any possible conflicts should be clearly recorded along with the decision reached in minuted meetings where they arise.

Probity

All members of the Society are required to maintain registration of the GMC or equivalent regulatory body with no restriction of practice and uphold relevant standards of probity. In particular we are required to act in an honest and trustworthy way when acting for, or interacting with, the Society.

Diversity & Inclusion

BSCOS actively seeks to uphold the principles of diversity and inclusion in all its activities. We seek to promote an inclusive practice and culture. Membership of the Society brings with it an expectation that these principles will be supported:

- We will work to eliminate any unlawful or unfair discrimination including direct or indirect discrimination, discrimination by association, discrimination linked to a perceived characteristic, harassment and victimisation.

- We will continue to strive towards a culture that is diverse and inclusive that recognises and develops the potential of all members and participants in our activities.

Meetings

1. Meetings will be conducted in an atmosphere of mutual respect.
2. Debate shall be honest and open.
3. Discussion shall be issue-centred rather than person-centred.
4. Etiquette:
    a. time keeping shall be respected.
    b. where necessary the Chair will identify a meeting to be quorate the start.
    c. speaking shall be through the Chair of the meeting.
    d. agenda items should be submitted to the secretary or chair by 2 weeks before an intimated meeting, with later items being at the discretion of the Chair.
    e. the Agenda will be issued at least 1 week before the meeting.
    f. there will be no side-discussions at the meeting.
    g. known absence from meeting shall be notified to the Chair in advance of the

meeting wherever possible.

h. the Chair of a meeting will be exempted from taking the minute.

5. Personal views should be clearly distinguished from collective decisions of a committee or group.

6. All contributions will be valued.

7. Any Member or attendee at a Society meeting or event who does not understand the purpose and emphasis of these ground rules shall be expected to seek clarification

8. Expenses shall be payable to Members acting on legitimate Board or subcommittee business within the rates set out and only when receipts are presented

Termination of membership

In the event of perceived misconduct of a member, the Board will follow the GMC principles of Good medical practice.

Membership of the society shall cease :

1. in the event of a member failing to pay the appropriate subscription in full within 3 months of the due date, that membership shall expire with immediate effect. Thereafter, a new formal application for membership would need to be submitted for readmission to the Society.

2. where professional registration is suspended by the General Medical Council or equivalent regulatory body for Affiliate members.

3. when a letter of resignation is sent to the secretary of the Society.

Appendix III: GDPR Policy

From 25th May 2018 the new General Data Protection Regulation came into force. This replaced the Data Protection Act of 1998 and is designed to give individuals more rights and protection regarding the use of their personal data by organisations.

BSCOS members are reminded that is their responsibility to protect access to the secure areas of the website by protecting their login and password and not to share such data with any other person.

BSCOS collects personal data from its members for several purposes:

- **Membership administration**
- **Online payments via Stripe**
- **Administration of the Society's annual meeting**

- **Keeping in touch with members by email**
- **Membership directory**
- **Surveys**

The full BSCOS Privacy Policy is available on the website. GDPR requires that individuals opt into the use of their data for some purposes and we therefore need to ask for consent for us to be able to send emails, to display details in the membership directory and to send the occasional survey.

We therefore ask that members keep their preferences up to date on the website. You may remove your consent at any time by using the update preferences link or by contacting webadmin@bscos.org.uk directly.

GENERAL PRIVACY NOTICE

How BSCOS ('we') use your information
BSCOS is committed to safeguarding your personal information. In order to handle 'personal data' about you we are required by law to provide this notice to you.

Your personal data – what is it?
"Personal data" is any information about a living individual which allows them to be identified from that data (for example a name, photographs, videos, email address, or address). Identification can be by the information alone or in conjunction with any other information. The processing of personal data is governed by *[the Data Protection Bill/Act 2017 the General Data Protection Regulation 2016/679 (the "GDPR" and other legislation relating to personal data and rights such as the Human Rights Act 1998]*.

Why are we collecting your data?
We collect personal data to provide appropriate membership services, to monitor and assess the quality of our services, to fulfil our purposes as a society and to comply with the law regarding data sharing. In legal terms

this is called 'legitimate interests'. When it is required, we may also ask you for your consent to process your data. We do not share your information with others except as described in this notice.

What data do we process?
When we hold or use your information it is known as 'processing'. We will process some or all of the following where necessary to fulfil our roles and responsibilities as a Society:

- Names, titles, and aliases, photographs;

- Contact details such as telephone numbers, addresses, and email addresses;

- Where they are relevant to our purposes, or where you provide them to us, we may process demographic information such as gender, age, date of birth, nationality, place of work, academic/professional qualifications;

- Where you make donations or pay for activities, financial identifiers such as bank account numbers, payment card numbers, payment/transaction identifiers, policy numbers, and claim numbers;

- Where you provide this information, we may also process data from the other categories of sensitive personal data (these are defined as: racial or ethnic origin, sex life, mental and physical health, details of injuries, medication/treatment received, political beliefs, labour union affiliation, genetic data, biometric data, data concerning sexual orientation and criminal records, fines and other similar judicial records). At present, however, BSCOS has no plans to utilise any data from these categories.

How do we process your personal data?
We will comply with legal obligations to keep personal data up to date; to store and destroy it securely; to not collect or retain excessive amounts of data; to keep personal data secure, and to protect personal data from loss, misuse, unauthorised access and disclosure and to ensure that appropriate technical measures are in place to protect personal data.

We use your personal data for some or all of the following purposes:

- To enable us to meet any legal and statutory obligations;

- To provide you with appropriate support and services;

- To act in line with our constitution;

- To administer the membership records;

- To provide a membership directory online and to allow communication between members of the Society;

- To fundraise and promote the interests of the Society;

- To maintain our own accounts and records;

- To process membership payments or payments for events;

- To seek your views or comments;

- To notify you of changes to our services and events;

- To send you communications which you have requested and that may be of interest to you. These may include information about campaigns, appeals, other fundraising activities;

- To process a grant or application for funding;

- To enable us to provide a voluntary service for the benefit of the public;

What is the legal basis for us processing your personal data?
Most of our data is processed because it is necessary for our legitimate interests, or the legitimate interests of a third party (such as a delegated data processing provider). We will always take into account your interests, rights and freedoms. Some of our processing may be necessary for compliance with a legal obligation. We may also process data if it is necessary for the performance of a contract

with you, or to take steps to enter into a contract.

Where your information is used other than in accordance with one of these legal bases, we will first obtain your consent to that use.

Sharing your personal data

Your personal data will be treated as strictly confidential. It will only be shared with third parties where it is legally required or where you first give us your prior consent. It is likely that we will need to share your data with some or all of the following (but only where necessary):

- Our agents and contractors. For example, we may ask a commercial provider to send out newsletters on our behalf, or to maintain our database software. At present our mailing list uses MailChimp (www.mailchimp.com), our membership database is provided by Sitelok (www.vibralogix.com/sitelok), membership payments are processed by Stripe (www.stripe.com/gb) and annual meeting payments are managed by Eventbrite (www.eventbrite.co.uk). All have appropriate security and privacy policies available on their websites;

• Other persons or organisations operating with permission within the Society;

• On occasion, other Societies with whom we are carrying out joint events or activities.

How long do we keep your personal data?
We will keep some records permanently if we are legally required to do so. We may keep some other records for an extended period of time. For example, it is current best practice to keep financial records for a minimum period of 7 years to support HMRC audits. In general, we will endeavour to keep data only for as long as we need it. This means that we may delete it when it is no longer needed.

Your rights and your personal data
You have the following rights with respect to your personal data: When exercising any of the rights listed below, in order to process your

request, we may need to verify your identity for your security. In such cases we will need you to respond with proof of your identity before you can exercise these rights.

1. The right to access information we hold on you

    a. At any point you can contact us to request the information we hold on you as well as why we   have that information, who has access to the information and where we obtained the   information from. Once we have received your request we will respond within one month.

    b. There are no fees or charges for the first request but additional requests for the same data may   be subject to an administrative fee.

2. The right to correct and update the information we hold on you

- If the data we hold on you is out of date, incomplete or incorrect, you can inform us, and your data will be updated. Alternatively, you may correct your own data using the Update Profile button when logged in to the website.

3. The right to have your information erased.

- If you feel that we should no longer be using your data or that we are illegally using your data, you can request that we erase the data we hold. When we receive your request, we will confirm whether the data has been deleted or the reason why it cannot be deleted (for example because we need it for our legitimate interests or regulatory purpose(s)).

4. The right to object to processing of your data

- You have the right to request that we stop processing your data. Upon receiving the request, we will contact you and let you know if we are able to comply or if we have legitimate grounds to continue to process your data. Even after you exercise your right to object, we may continue to hold your data to comply with your other rights or to bring or defend legal claims.

5. The right to data portability

- You have the right to request that we transfer some of your data to another controller. We will comply with your request, where it is feasible to do so, within one month of receiving your request.

6. The right to withdraw your consent to the processing at any time for any processing of data to which consent was sought.

- You can withdraw your consent easily by email at webadmin@bscos.org.uk, or by post (to the Secretary via the British Orthopaedic Association, 35-43 Lincoln's Inn Fields, London WC2A 3PE).

7. The right to object to the processing of personal data where applicable.

8. The right to lodge a complaint with the Information Commissioner's Office.

Transfer of Data Abroad
Any electronic personal data transferred to

countries or territories outside the EU will only be placed on systems complying with measures giving equivalent protection of personal rights either through international agreements or contracts approved by the European Union. Our website is also accessible from overseas so on occasion some personal data (for example in a newsletter) may be accessed from overseas.

Further processing

If we wish to use your personal data for a new purpose, not covered by this Notice, then we will provide you with a new notice explaining this new use prior to commencing the processing and setting out the relevant purposes and processing conditions. Where and whenever necessary, we will seek your prior consent to the new processing.

Contact Details

Please contact us if you have any questions about this Privacy Notice or the information we hold about you or to exercise all relevant rights, queries or complaints:

By email at webadmin@bscos.org.uk or

c/o The Secretary to the BSCOS Board, British Orthopaedic Association, 35-43 Lincoln's Inn Fields, London WC2A 3PE

You can contact the Information Commissioners Office on 0303 123 1113 or via email https://ico.org.uk/global/contact-us/email/ or at the Information Commissioner's Office, Wycliffe House, Water Lane, Wilmslow, Cheshire SK9 5AF.

Acknowledgements

Sincere thanks go to the following members of the Society for their contributions to make this volume possible: *Colin Bruce, Tony Catterall, Deborah Eastwood, James Fernandes, James Robb, Keith Tucker, and the late Richard Montgomery...*

...as well as the current Board of BSCOS who are a selfless team who have worked consistently hard for the Society during my tenure as president: *Guy Atherton, John Cashman, Simon Thomas, Ed Bache, Rob Freeman, Darius Rad, Marcos Katchburian, Adelle Fishlock, Helen Bryant, Phil Henman.*

Personal thanks are due to my own mentors, John Spencer (Guy's, London) and Tom Scotland (RACH, Aberdeen) who in turn taught me the art of surgery and to love our amazing subspecialty.

I am finally grateful beyond measure to my ever patient wife, *Pam* and daughters, *Emily and Grace*, for bearing with my endless editing antics.

For the inevitable errors and omissions I can only offer sincere apologies and the assurance that the best was done with the information available. I entrust their correction to a future colleague upon a future happy anniversary of our Society!

SB

Bibliography

Children's Orthopaedics in North America –
History, Genealogy, and Evolution
Dennis R Wenger
POSNA, Chicago, 2006
10 0-9779151-0-7

Operations that made History
Harold Ellis
Greenwich Medical Media, 1996
1 900151 154

BSCOS – The first 40 years